Reconceptualising the Moral Economy of Criminal Justice

DOI: 10.1057/9781137468468.0001

Other Palgrave Pivot titles

Thomas Kaiserfeld: **Beyond Innovation: Technology, Institution and Change as Categories for Social Analysis**

Dirk Jacob Wolfson: **The Political Economy of Sustainable Development: Valuation, Distribution, Governance**

Twyla J. Hill: **Family Caregiving in Aging Populations**

Alexander M. Stoner and Andony Melathopoulos: **Freedom in the Anthropocene: Twentieth Century Helplessness in the Face of Climate Change**

Christine J. Hong: **Identity, Youth, and Gender in the Korean American Christian Church**

Cenap Çakmak and Murat Ustaoğlu: **Post-Conflict Syrian State and Nation Building: Economic and Political Development**

Richard J. Arend: **Wicked Entrepreneurship: Defining the Basics of Entreponerology**

Rubén Arcos and Randolph H. Pherson (editors): **Intelligence Communication in the Digital Era: Transforming Security, Defence and Business**

Jane Chapman, Dan Ellin and Adam Sherif: **Comics, the Holocaust and Hiroshima**

AKM Ahsan Ullah, Mallik Akram Hossain and Kazi Maruful Islam: **Migration and Worker Fatalities Abroad**

Debra Reddin van Tuyll, Nancy McKenzie Dupont and Joseph R. Hayden: **Journalism in the Fallen Confederacy**

Michael Gardiner: **Time, Action and the Scottish Independence Referendum**

Tom Bristow: **The Anthropocene Lyric: An Affective Geography of Poetry, Person, Place**

Shepard Masocha: **Asylum Seekers, Social Work and Racism**

Michael Huxley: **The Dancer's World, 1920–1945: Modern Dancers and Their Practices Reconsidered**

Michael Longo and Philomena Murray: **Europe's Legitimacy Crisis: From Causes to Solutions**

Mark Lauchs, Andy Bain and Peter Bell: **Outlaw Motorcycle Gangs: A Theoretical Perspective**

Majid Yar: **Crime and the Imaginary of Disaster: Post-Apocalyptic Fictions and the Crisis of Social Order**

Sharon Hayes and Samantha Jeffries: **Romantic Terrorism: An Auto-Ethnography of Domestic Violence, Victimization and Survival**

Gideon Maas and Paul Jones: **Systemic Entrepreneurship: Contemporary Issues and Case Studies**

DOI: 10.1057/9781137468468.0001

palgrave▸pivot

Reconceptualising the Moral Economy of Criminal Justice: A New Perspective

Philip Whitehead

Reader in Criminal and Social Justice, University of Teesside, UK

palgrave
macmillan

DOI: 10.1057/9781137468468.0001

First published 2015 by
PALGRAVE MACMILLAN

Palgrave Macmillan in the UK is an imprint of Macmillan Publishers Limited, registered in England, company number 785998, of Houndmills, Basingstoke, Hampshire RG21 6XS.

Palgrave Macmillan in the US is a division of St Martin's Press LLC, 175 Fifth Avenue, New York, NY 10010.

Palgrave Macmillan is the global academic imprint of the above companies and has companies and representatives throughout the world.

Palgrave® and Macmillan® are registered trademarks in the United States, the United Kingdom, Europe and other countries.

ISBN: 978–1–137–46847–5 EPUB
ISBN: 978–1–137–46846–8 PDF
ISBN: 978–1–137–46845–1 Hardback

A catalogue record for this book is available from the British Library.

A catalog record for this book is available from the Library of Congress.

www.palgrave.com/pivot

DOI: 10.1057/9781137468468

Contents

DOI: 10.1057/9781137468468.0001

Foreword

The Teesside Centre for Realist Criminology opened its doors in September 2013. Our goal in establishing the centre was to facilitate theoretical and empirical research that engages honestly with the serious social problems we face today. We were tired of the unworldly idealism that continues to dominate leftist criminology yet we had little time for a-theoretical state-centred administrative criminology. Why, we wondered, did dusty old ideas from the 1960s continue to dominate our discipline when cognate fields were driving forward new accounts of reality at a fair pace? In an era defined by the economic crisis of 2008 and its aftermath, why were criminologists failing to look again at the inevitable harms of global capitalism? Why were they still droning on about moral panics? Was a growing percentage of the western population not falling into debt peonage? Was the gap between rich and poor not widening at a staggering rate, leaving growing numbers dependent upon soup kitchens and food banks while others indulged in the most obscene forms of conspicuous consumption? Was the economic development of eastern economies not built upon unacceptably exploitative labour practices? Does ecological change not threaten to transform our world in the near future as global warming precipitates further conflict and violence? We hoped to build a new leftist criminology that took harm seriously, that moved beyond left idealism and left realism to delve beneath our experience of social reality to discover new truths worthy of attention about the neoliberal system and the forces that drive it forward.

DOI: 10.1057/9781137468468.0002

In 2015, we were very proud to hand over the directorship of the Teesside Centre for Realist Criminology to Philip Whitehead, our colleague and the author of this book. Philip was a natural fit for the centre, and we are sure that the centre will continue to advance under his stewardship. Here he has a dramatic story to tell of the marketisation of the Probation Service and the meek capitulation of politics to the logic of neoliberal managerialism. After many years working in this institution, Philip is understandably aggrieved at what has happened. Human contact and care-giving have been abandoned in the name of efficiency and value for money, and the institutional transformation of the Probation Service tells us much about the broader transformation of social life and the severing of obligations to others in an era in which the market economy's intrusion into our social institutions has become a fait accompli. A sense of loss and diminishment runs through this book, and that is entirely fitting given its context.

However, Philip does a wonderful job of shedding new light on these transformations. In particular, he attempts to rethink the concept of moral economy and use it as a platform for vigorous critique. While most accounts of change in the criminal justice system focus on administrative processes and governmental policies to offer well-aimed but limited critiques of what they like to call 'nuances and complexities', Philip acknowledges these details but moves beyond them to construct a thoroughgoing philosophical critique that eschews small-scale reformism and holds out the prospect of starting again, of building a new criminal justice system on a foundation of morality and a sense of obligation to others.

We are sure that you will find much here of great value. Perhaps more than ever criminology needs to rediscover its theoretical ambition. It needs to cast aside restrictive concerns about objectivity and balance and once again construct detailed, thoughtful and innovative critiques of harm and injustice. Philip's work will, we're sure, be of significant importance for those who wish to develop nuanced and theoretically sophisticated accounts of the world as it is today, but it will be absolutely vital for those keen to understand the forces that are driving the transformation of our criminal justice system and other public institutions. We warmly welcome you to this book. We hope you enjoy it as much as we have.

Simon Winlow and Steve Hall
Founders of the Teesside Centre for Realist
Criminology, May 2015

DOI: 10.1057/9781137468468.0002

Acknowledgements

Books may bear the name of a single author, but the writing process requires support and encouragement. I'm intellectually indebted to Steve Hall, Simon Winlow and other academic colleagues in the Teesside Centre for Realist Criminology. David Faulkner, Roger Statham and Evi Boukli read the work in progress, and their comments were invaluable. I'm acutely mindful of the environment required at home to read and write and, for nearly four decades, Carolyn has provided this. Alex, Tim and Jenny contribute more than they realise when they come home. Nothing I say can adequately express my love and gratitude.

DOI: 10.1057/9781137468468.0003

Prologue

After working in a hostel for ex-offenders during 1978–79, then training as a social worker of the criminal and civil courts at Lancaster University during 1979–81, I was employed as a probation officer in the north-east of England from July 1981 to November 2007.[1] Since then I've acquired the status of a semi-detached but increasingly troubled observer of organisational torments and ideological contortions. Probation, an organisation in, but not always of, the criminal justice system, has not suddenly acquired a death drive. Rather, it has become the depersonalised object of a coercive politics of destructive interference imposed from above, shunted into the market sphere, scythed down and relegated into the twilight zone. It is as though the past never happened as historical tradition and accumulated ethico-cultural deposits count for nothing, consumed by the reign of the modernisers in an almost final act of petulant destruction.

The purpose and scope of this monograph not only theorises, reconceptualises, but also refines the concept of moral economy in its relevance for, and application to, criminal justice in England and Wales with specific reference to probation. Beginning in the 1980s, followed by successive New Labour administrations from 1997 (Whitehead and Statham, 2006; Whitehead, 2010) and the Transforming Rehabilitation agenda of 2010–15, criminal justice has been seized by the technical requirements of economy and efficiency, value for money, measurable outcomes, punishment, prisons and bureaucratic rationality. These features have combined to impose a paradigm shift in governmental policies and organisational practices, indexed most notably in probation. The vital contribution of this monograph advances the argument that criminal justice cannot be reduced to an instrumentally driven operation to achieve fiscal efficiencies or provide investment opportunities to the commercial sector. Rather, the starting point is to establish its intellectual and moral foundations, the precepts of which are required to legitimate policy and practice. Accordingly, the concept of moral economy constitutes a point of rupture to the parvenu orthodoxy of criminal and penal policy, its modernising blandishments and the platform of neoliberal ideological and material interests that it reflects and reproduces (Hall, 2012; Reiner, 2007; Wacquant, 2009). This is not another book that describes criminal justice functions (see Davies et al., 2010) because it takes the decisive but contested step to reenergise thinking on morality that has atrophied. Moral economy is foregrounded as an analytical category conducive to excavating discernible transformations; it functions as a conceptual device; it also makes a serious contribution to the urgent task of reconstruction. Moral economy can bear the weight of these heavy demands placed upon it, as well as constructing a platform on which to plot a different way of thinking about doing justice. What has emerged during the period between 1979 and 2015 has not been inevitable, any more than the future is determined to repeat the past.

Before exploring moral economy and putting it to work, it is necessary to assemble some of the intellectual resources on the moral domain by raiding a number of academic disciplines appertaining to philosophy and theology, personalism, psychoanalysis, the great transformation signalled by the Industrial Age and social theory. This is by no means a comprehensive but selective treatment to facilitate theoretical interrogation. Although these diverse academic disciplines are unquestionably informative, they are assembled in the first chapter preparatory to elucidating the content of, and argument for, moral economy in Chapter 2. I want to explain why it should matter, whilst being mindful of its complex and contested character. It will then be possible to apply moral economy to events within criminal justice between 1979 and 2010 in Chapter 3, and the Rehabilitation Revolution between 2010 and 2015 in Chapter 4. Finally, Chapter 5 reanimates interest in morality following the latest bout of privatising public assets. It is imperative to ask: who is responsible for the moral dynamic in what is an increasingly market-driven criminal justice system when investment opportunities assume

DOI: 10.1057/9781137468468.0004

greater significance than services to offenders, and when the state has ceded its responsibilities to privatised solutions: the probation residue, the 21 Community Rehabilitation Companies announced on the 29 October 2014, restorative justice, community chaplaincy, the voluntary sector? Finding answers to these questions is urgent because Burrow, when evaluating the evidence of moral decline in classical antiquity, comments: 'The past was unlike the present not only in superficial material terms, but morally and intellectually. They did things differently then, and thought and felt differently' (2009, 115).

A warning: one should feel nauseous at zealous moralising because it has a nasty habit of lapsing into self-righteous bigotry, an unseemly human trait. By contrast, citizens in a πόλις (polis) have a responsibility to ask searching question about what is right, what constitutes the good society, what is fair and just, not only within primary human relationships but organisational functions, political economy and, in this monograph, the criminal justice system. These fundamental questions can be traced to the beginning of Western philosophy with Socrates on virtue (αρέτη aretē), Plato on justice (δικαιοσύνη dikaiosunē) and Aristotle on ethics and eudaimonism (εὐδαιμονια).[2] For far too long these foundational intellectual and moral questions have been ignored by government and those who should provide moral leadership rather than managerial expertise in the criminal justice system. Criminal justice is more important than the latest managerial and administrative gimmickry, technical rationality and strangulated bureaucratic procedures. If, for Aristotle (2000), human beings require a function, which is to live according to the virtues that lead to happiness, according to Schweitzer the function of humanity is expressed as reverence for life which constitutes the basic principle of the moral. This is a suitable place to begin this enquiry, not least because Schweitzer is hardly ever cited on the subject of moral philosophy. An interest in his work should be reanimated.

Notes

1   Probation chronology: 1977–78 probation volunteer in Lancaster; 1978–79 Hostel for ex-offenders in Lancaster; September 1979 to June 1981 social work training at Lancaster University; July 1981–87 probation officer, Middlesbrough; 1987–93 Research and Information Officer; 1993–99 Middlesbrough Court Team; 1999–2001 probation officer, Redcar; 2001–05

DOI: 10.1057/9781137468468.0004

Senior Practice Development Assessor to Trainee Probation Officers. Finally, from 2005 to November 2007 at South Bank probation office, Teesside Magistrates' and Crown Courts and the Hartlepool Magistrates' Court.

2 See Kenny (2010: 206) where he discusses the Socratic virtues of piety, temperance, fortitude and justice in the *Republic* (Plato 1974). Furthermore, Plato's concept of justice (δικαιοσύνη) is worthwhile for its own sake (*Republic* 358b–62c). It is deemed beneficial to those who possess it because it conduces to psychic health. We shall return to Socrates, Plato and Aristotle later.

DOI: 10.1057/9781137468468.0004

1
Theorising Morality: Assembling the Intellectual Resources

Abstract: *This chapter assembles some of the intellectual resources to introduce, explore critically and theorise the moral. To pursue this task it is necessary to allude to a rich compendium of philosophical ethics; theological and Christological insights; the doctrine of personalism; psychoanalysis and symbolic ethics. Furthermore, after considering politico-economic and moral conditions before and after the great transformation of the late-18th century, specific references to moral economy are introduced before turning briefly to social theory.*

Whitehead, Philip. *Reconceptualising the Moral Economy of Criminal Justice: A New Perspective.* Basingstoke: Palgrave Macmillan, 2015. DOI: 10.1057/9781137468468.0005.

Philosophical ethics

Although Albert Schweitzer (from 14 January 1875 to 4 September 1965) demonstrated little academic precocity during his formative years, he cultivated a respect for life that shaped his ethical thought. By the age of 30 he had obtained doctorates in philosophy, theology and music, prior to studying medicine to work as a missionary at Lambaréné, Gabon, in French Equatorial Africa. Seaver commented that after Schweitzer had distinguished himself in the philosophy of Kant, the interpretation of Bach and Biblical scholarship, 'behold him now, in a shed by a riverside in Equatorial Africa, holding, with a comrade's grip, the hand of a primitive negro whom his surgical skill had just rescued from an agonizing death' (1947: 60). His primary intellectual outputs in the aforementioned fields that can be added to his first doctorate on *The Religious Philosophy of Kant* are cited below.[1] The text requiring close attention is *Civilisation and Ethics* Part II (1929), because it purviews Hellenistic ethics, the Judaeo-Christian inheritance, continuing through Renaissance and Enlightenment moral perspectives and beyond into the nineteenth century.[2] His primary concern was the tragedy of the Western world-view that collapsed with the First World War when barbarism on an industrial scale destroyed the promise of the European Enlightenment for progress towards human civilisation through reason (Outram, 2013). Furthermore, the encroaching gloom of technical rationality and bureaucratic state-craft (Weber, 1922/1968), quantifiable state-istics (Cullen, 1975), positivistic obsessions and cost–benefit analysis combined to erode the ethico-cultural and emotional dynamics of existence (Meštrović, 1997). By the spring of 1923 the first two volumes of *Philosophy of Civilisation* were complete, but Part II constitutes the coping stone and supreme achievement of his work (Seaver, 1947: 85) as it explores the quest for the foundational principle of the moral. The question of ethics is different to figuring out the *world-process* that speculates on the ontological structure of reality with, for example, Plato and Hegel. Schweitzer followed Kant rather than Hegel by questioning whether it is possible to discover a world-process explicated, for example, as Spirit's growing self-consciousness. Accordingly, metaphysical certitudes are beyond the power of abstract thought to comprehend so that 'the more systematized any philosophical system is (for example, the immensely imposing systems of an Aristotle or a Hegel) so much the more fallacious it can be shown to be' (Seaver, 1947: 280). Schweitzer's agnosticism

DOI: 10.1057/9781137468468.0005

towards metaphysical system-building and theoretical abstraction is replaced with an enthusiasm for life. Not the Cartesian 'I think, therefore I am', but rather 'I am life that wills to live' as the starting point for *reverence for life*. It is elucidated that 'Reverence for Life pretends to no knowledge of the world or of what the world may mean; it formulates no world-view' (Seaver, 1947: 293) but advances a life-view. Reverence for life is not constitutive of speculative reason but practical reason that affirms the sacredness of existence which is universal in its demand and scope. Consequently, Schweitzer issued a practical invitation to 'Find yourselves some secondary work, an inconspicuous one, perhaps a secret one. Open your eyes and look for a human being or some work devoted to human welfare which needs from someone a little time or friendliness, a little sympathy, or sociability, or work' (1929: 260). Schweitzer does not advance a critique of 19th century liberal capitalism throughout his ethical enquiries. Nevertheless, he tangentially analyses its effects when issuing the summons for the restoration of ethical responsibility that affirms life per se which has implications for politico-economic structures. In fact, he questions how it is possible to attain the standard of economic justice unless it is premised upon the morality of reverence for life (1929: 277). Even after the calamitous capitalist crisis of 2007/08, we still need to arrive at an accommodation of how to organise ourselves morally. It is as urgent now as when Schweitzer was writing.

Schweitzer's exposition of Kantian morality confirms human beings as ends rather than means, an interest in motives rather than consequences, so that the 'utilitarian ethic must abdicate before that of immediate and sovereign duty' (1929: 107). Kant's deontological ethic opposes utilitarianism in asseverating that human beings are intrinsically worthy of respect, so the basic principle of ethics transcends contingent conditions and political manipulation. What is more, the moral impulse as the imperative of duty intimates a transcendent realm that cannot be known, only postulated. Because of the limits placed on knowledge, religious experience is reduced to the moral impulse. God belongs to the numinous not phenomenal realm which is beyond the scope of human knowledge, yet in whom human beings believe to act morally out of practical reason. Kant asserted that just because something facilitates pleasure or Aristotelian happiness does not make it right: 'A good will is not good because of what it effects or accomplishes. Even if... this will is entirely lacking in power to carry out its intentions, if by its utmost effort it still accomplishes nothing... even then it would still shine like a jewel for its own sake as something which has its full value in itself' (1785/2005: 65). Schweitzer's criticism of Kant is that even though there is merit in universally binding duty, it lacks human content: 'How far Kant is from understanding the problem of finding a basic moral principle which has a definite content can be seen from the fact that he never gets beyond an utterly narrow conception of the ethical' (1929: 108). In doing so Kant does not establish a basic principle of the moral that encapsulates the whole of life-existence in not allowing for sympathy as a springboard of ethics. Therefore, the Kantian position elevates rigid duty above Aristotelian happiness, Enlightenment reason before human sympathy and emotion. During Schweitzer's historical exposition and critique, ethical systems are allocated to one of three positions (1929: 72).

First, egoism can be transposed into altruism by meditation or psychological reflection to benefit others. Second, altruism is imposed onto individuals because, according to Hobbes, they predominantly act out of self-interest – man as wolf to man. Although the Aristotle– Augustine–Aquinas philosophical and theological tradition asserted the natural sociability of human beings who are suited for life in the polis (Pagden, 2013: 44), Hobbes rejected this for a pessimistic anthropology that must be restrained by a central political authority to ensure social co-existence. Third, egoism and altruism are constitutive components of the human condition and, where the latter is concerned, it is out of sympathy for others that benevolence arises. At this point it is of interest to note that Hutcheson, influenced by Shaftesbury, postulated a *moral sense* that is able to differentiate between ethical and unethical behaviour in others. Moreover, Hume, influenced by, yet proceeding beyond Hutcheson, asserted that reason was insufficient to provide instruction on matters of blame or approbation. Sentiment is required which 'can be no other than a *feeling* for the happiness of mankind, and a resentment of their misery...' (Hume, 1777/1983: 83 italics added). Accordingly, Schweitzer summarised that ethical systems have been deemed a matter of reason or rational deduction; the intimation of a transcendental realm (Kant); imposed by a central authority to estab- lish sociality (Hobbes); a biologically endowed moral sense that can be added to the five physical senses (Hutcheson). Ethics overlaps with politics, anthropology, psychology, sociology and education. There is also the conundrum of whether it is a biological-given or something we repeatedly have to learn (nature or nurture)? More recently Michael Sandel (2009) advanced a philosophico-political perspective on morality and justice according to three positions: utilitarianism, liberal economics and Aristotelian virtue ethics. Eagleton (2009) covers some of the ground contained in Schweitzer (1929), Sandel (2009) and MacIntyre (1967), but assigns ethical systems to one of three psychic orders that we shall come to later. Schneewind (2003) is indispensable on the subject of moral philosophy.

Pagden contributes to this discussion when arguing that the aim of the European Enlightenment was *civilisation*, defined as a 'process of aggregation and cooperation – the working out in time of the "sympathy" which bound all human beings inexorably to one another' (2013: 210). This interpretation envisaged that reason would improve the world through scientific advances, the declaration of universal justice and human rights, establishing minimal ethical standards and the moral duty to alleviate suffering. Whatever the prospects for civilisation in the 18th century Age of Reason, they were buffeted by industrial capitalism in the 19th century with its laissez faire economics, utilitarian philosophy, Hobbesian atomistic individualism that pitted self-interest over public interest, profit before social well-being and capitalist exchange relations before Aristotelian virtue. Pagden, like Schweitzer, does not adequately address the problematic of liberal capitalism in his exposition of the Enlightenment vision of a benign, unified and cosmopolitan humanity in what increasingly became a modern and post-theological European world. He explains that 'Hobbes had not merely demolished the Aristotelian–Thomist theological order, he had also banished any possibility of any mode of human interaction which was not based upon a crude calculation of interests' (2013: 55). But where was Humean feeling in this bleak dystopian view of humanity? Are we nothing more than biological and psychological beings ineluctably stuck with the tyranny of our selfish egos, pursuing our own interests and in constant conflict with the social? Pufendorf, with Shaftesbury, Hutcheson, even Adam Smith, appealed to sentiment, human beings as moral creatures, with inclinations and feelings of benevolence, the self's recognition of someone other than themselves that transcended Hobbes and Grotius (Schneewind, 2003). This is not the language of Kant's rigid duty and the categorical imperative, but it does provide content for Schweitzer's ethic of reverence for life. Throughout all these discussions on the moral and content of ethical systems, Pagden asserts optimistically that there was a demand for a theory of human mind that incorporated a richer account of the human person than one governed by instrumental and calculating

DOI: 10.1057/9781137468468.0005

self-interest, or even rigid duty, that was central to Schweitzer's ethic of reverence for life.

One of the unquestionable guarantors of morality for centuries was a God-orientated world-view, a philosophico-theological perspective. Charles Taylor (2007) argued that from the Fathers of the early Church, through to Augustine and Aquinas who supported a God-centred universe, it was axiomatic to believe in God. However, Renaissance science, post-Enlightenment secular philosophy and Nietzsche's proclamation of the 'death of god' disturbed this view. Nevertheless, this did not culminate in a final obituary notice posted on the history of God or study of moral philosophy. David Hume and Bertrand Russell, for example, may well have decoupled metaphysics from morality which rearranged the intellectual, religious and moral furniture, but the furniture remained, if less secure than formerly. Former certainties were intellectually challenged, but we still do not live in a 'Fatherless World' (Pagden's reference to Adam Smith, 1759/2009: 277; also Eagleton, 2014). This is a propitious moment to turn from philosophy to the former 'queen of sciences', namely theology. Raines suggests, 'In the twenty-first century, religion promises to be a major historical force for the first time in four hundred years' (2002: 12). Although Raines does not consign religion to a Freudian illusion, he fails to tell us whether it is a force for good or evil.

Theological and Christological ethics

On Being A Christian (Küng, 1977) is an academic though accessible text on theology and Christology with implications for theorising the moral. Küng's God (Θεός Theos) is not an object alongside objects in the world that can be known, empirically verified or accessible to pure reason. Kant and Schweitzer would approve. Instead, God is a proposition of faith, presupposed if human beings want to live a meaningfully moral life. To construct a language that makes it possible to talk about God (the primary task of theology), in conjunction with morality, is ontologically and epistemologically problematic. Moreover, theoretical reason and abstract speculative metaphysics of the Platonic and Hegelian sort are not all that useful as a guide for formulating a life-view. We are therefore shunted, as an existential necessity, onto more solid ground with Küng's exposition of Jesus of Nazareth as the definitive expression of God's cause

DOI: 10.1057/9781137468468.0005

in the world (God's logos – λόγος word), the anthropological exemplar who stands at the head of a restructured humanity. Schweitzer believed that the gift bestowed by Christianity is an ethic of self-renunciation to benefit others. By stripping back the accretions of church councils and their impenetrable dogmatic formulations (Kelly, 1968), centuries of religious conflict, byzantine ecclesiastical operations and priestly castes engaged in debilitating discussions on homosexuality, women priests and bishops, Jesus of Nazareth is the criterion of what it means to be human and to live humanely. This historical figure represents a 'Wholly new approach to life, at an awareness transformed from the roots upward, a new basic attitude, a different scale of values, a radical rethinking and returning of the whole man' (Küng, 1977: 546). From the prophetic literature on social justice (Jones, 1968), the ethical injunction to individual and community responsibility, and the resolution of disputes contained in the Old Testament literature; to the new covenant of neighbourliness and love extended to enemies (see the Ethical Lists in Metzger and Coogan, 1993: 201); the Judaeo-Christian inheritance provides a resource for exploring the concept of the moral. The Pauline inheritance is particularly important.

We must always keep in mind that Paul was a man of his own classical era, who's framing (or re-framing) of Christianity reflected his Greek, Roman and Jewish cultural inheritance. Pauline theology articulates the contours of a new humanity that, in turn, constitutes a new ethical community that requires explanation. When doing so it is necessary to allude to a considerable work of scholarship (Blumenfeld, 2001) that grounds Pauline theology and Christology within the intellectual parameters of Platonic and Aristotelian politics, and the literature known as the Pythagorean pseudepigrapha. The importance of Blumenfeld's scholarship is that it draws attention to the neglected political dynamic of the Pauline literature. It is not easy to produce a summation of this comprehensive and sometimes complex text but it demonstrates how Paul, in the style of Aristotelian *Ethics* (2000), moves from the individual to the polis (πόλις), ethics to politics. Like Aristotle 'Paul connects one's proper end with the collective end, the good of one with that of the many, ethics with politics' (Blumenfeld, 2001: 382), of which the epistolary motif is the one Body (soma σῶμα) with its interconnected limbs. What is good or moral is rooted in the concept of dikaiosunē (δικαιοσύνη justice), the opposite of adikia (ἀδικία injustice); it eschews evil, considers others and is universal in scope. It supports the Aristotelian virtues of wisdom,

DOI: 10.1057/9781137468468.0005

prudence and justice, but agapē (ἀγάπη love) is the essence of the new order within the polis (πόλις) that defines citizenship and civic order. The conception of the new political and ethical order eradicates the binaries between Jew and Greek, Greek and barbarian, free and slave, wealthy and poor and ruler and ruled within the transformed polis which is good news (το euangelion, τό εὐαγγέλιον). It does not invite monastic withdrawal into deserted landscapes but full engagement with the world to renew and transform it which is subversive, radical, scandalous, even revolutionary (see Milbank, 2010). The symbolic representation of the new existence is a disturbing cross (stauros σταυρός). In other words, at the beginning of Christianity is a sacrificial death that challenges anthropological self-interest. The sacrificial cross is the ultimate ethical expression of costly self-renunciation on behalf of the other, more convincing than doctrines of the atonement obsessed with haematology (Dillistone, 1982). Consequently, Pauline ethics echo Hippodamos and Aristotle who warn 'against social inequity and even economic surfeit, and the changes to sociality and social stability they present' (Blumenfeld, 2001: 388).[3] N.T. Wright, a former Bishop of Durham, explains that the scandalon of the New Testament presented in Pauline epistolary writing is that the new being in Christ 'overturns all the social pride and convention of the surrounding culture' (2009: 26). Human existence is transformed by faith by a new narrative and signification system. The wisdom of the world is not God's wisdom and 'the whole point of the gospel is to put the world – not upside down, because that is where it already is, but the right way up' (Wright, 2009: 131). Everything is judged by different political and ethical criteria that demand a new perspective on all dimensions of life that reconcile politics, ethics and anthropology into a transcendent unity.

Earlier I called for the reanimation of academic interest in the life and work of Albert Schweitzer. I now make a similar case for Dietrich Bonhoeffer on whom there is also a considerable primary and secondary literature.[4] Born in Breslau on the 4 February 1906 into a cultured, patriotic but not nationalistic family (Kelly and Nelson, 2003), the Bonhoeffer family moved to Berlin in 1912 when their father accepted the chair in psychiatry and nervous diseases at Berlin University. In 1919, following the death of an older brother in the First World War, Dietrich Bonhoeffer attended the Grunewald Gymnasium to continue his formative education. He later continued his studies in Tübingen before returning to Berlin to study theology, completing his doctorate when

DOI: 10.1057/9781137468468.0005

he was 21: *Sanctorum Communio*. In 1928, he spent a year in Barcelona as assistant pastor to a German-speaking Lutheran congregation: 'He would see how the so-called other half lived, meeting and spending time with people whose businesses had failed, with victims of poverty and crime, and with truly desperate individuals, as well as with bona fide criminals' (Metaxas, 2010: 78). Back in Berlin in 1929 he continued post-doctoral studies to qualify as a university lecturer – *Act and Being*. 'In Act and Being, he used philosophical language to show that theology is not merely another branch of philosophy, but something else entirely' (2010: 89). He was appointed assistant lecturer at Berlin University prior to visiting the United States for the first time during 1930–31 to study at Union Theological Seminary, New York. Not only was he aware of the Jewish situation in Germany, but also racism against black people in America. He returned home in June 1931 by which time 'Bonhoeffer was not interested in intellectual abstraction. Theology must lead to the practical aspects of how to live as a Christian' (2010: 129).

The rise of Hitler during the 1930s was the context within which Bonhoeffer proceeded from theoretical abstraction to a practical ethic of human maturity and responsibility. The Bonhoeffer family was entangled in the struggle against the Nazi state and Dietrich asserted the theological position that morality is the unconditional obligation to and for others, just as the church is only the church when it exists for others. Nazi ideology perverted history and truth through pursuing a Nietzschean will to power to which the Confessing Church was an ethical response. During 1934–35 Bonhoeffer served as pastor in London to two German congregations, at Sydenham and the East End, and at the end of this period accepted the directorship of the Confessing Church in Germany which facilitated the creation of Finkenwalde seminary before being closed by the Gestapo. On the 4 June 1939 he temporarily returned to New York, but was back in Berlin by the 27 July. He decided he could not remain in the United States in circumstances of conflict afflicting his own country. In his departing letter he stated that 'I will have no right to participate in the reconstruction of Christian life in Germany after the war if I do not share the trials of this time with my people' (Kelly and Nelson, 2003: 27). In 1940 Bonhoeffer was invited to join the *Abwehr* as cover for resistance work and continued to work on *Ethics*. He was involved in Operation 7 to save a contingent of Jews and, by February 1942, Dohnanyi was aware that the Gestapo was watching him and Bonhoeffer. They were arrested on the 5 April 1943 and the next 18 months were spent at Tegel prison, but at this juncture the state was not aware of his involvement in a conspiracy to kill Hitler. His circumstances dramatically changed after the failed Stauffenberg bomb plot in July 1944 that implicated Bonhoeffer and, on 8 October 1944, was taken from Tegel to the Gestapo prison at Prinz-Albrecht Strasse. On the 7 February 1945 he was transferred to Buchenwald concentration camp where he spent the next seven weeks. Then from Buchenwald to Flossenburg for possibly only 12 hours before being tried and executed on the order of Hitler at dawn on 9 April 1945. Bonhoeffer did not advance an immature theology of a God who rescues people from their problems (*deus ex machina*), a supernatural chemist's shop which remedies every human complaint. This is religion not Christianity. On the contrary, 'For Bonhoeffer, Christian faith demands that we accept God's own vulnerability in embracing those to whom society deals destructive poverty, vicious enslavement, and malicious neglect' (Kelly and Nelson, 2003: 177). Bonhoeffer's theology is rooted in Pauline justice and equality, the expression of responsible action to and for others in a world come of age.

Dumas (1971: 139) said that Bonhoeffer considered *Ethics* (1955) his magnum opus in which he argued that the reality of God revealed in Jesus of Nazareth is the starting point for Christian ethics. The ethical demand calls for 'the complete surrender of one's own life to the other man. Only the selfless man lives responsibly, and this means that only the selfless man *lives*' (Bonhoeffer, 1955: 225). This ethic opposes egoism and the pathway advocated by the Nietzschean Übermensch who inverts Christian morality beyond the proclamation of the 'death of God' by trampling over others with disdain. Bonhoeffer agreed with Schweitzer that this has implications for our understanding of human existence, the sense we have of self and cognitive–emotional engagement with others, the judgements we formulate and decisions we make about how we organise ourselves alongside each other. Furthermore, the church can only claim to be the church when it exists for others, which it sometimes spectacularly fails to do when *some* of its leaders and members inflict damage on others by engaging in behaviours that betray the essence of their vocation. Instead of the church being the human community as it is intended to be where relationships are structured by agapē (ἀγάπη), it behaves like any other fallible organisation in falling short of its primary task. According to Bonhoeffer, participation in the sufferings of God in the midst of the world is more than an ethical response of solidarity with the weak and poor. It is, as he theologically expressed it in *Ethics*

DOI: 10.1057/9781137468468.0005

'participation in the indivisible whole of the divine reality' (Dumas, 1971: 191). This theologico-anthropological construction asserts that true freedom can only be found in turning towards to the neighbour in a basic act of moral and social solidarity and equality by losing oneself, not the pursuit of stupid and ephemeral pleasures as the acme of indulgent self-interest at the expense of others; not self-aggrandisement but self-renunciation. As stated towards the end of his life in *Letters and Papers from Prison* (during 1943–44): 'Consequently the Christian is called to follow the reality of Jesus Christ in his godforsakeness in the midst of the world come of age, so that the world can be "re-structured" – a word preferable to the religiously coloured word "saved"' (Dumas, 1971: 197).

The resources assembled so far constitute philosophical, theological and Christological reflections on the moral. For Schweitzer, Küng and Bonhoeffer, ethics is not the rigid application of duty, nor the subject of speculative reason. Rather, it is a practical reason of refined and mature sensibility, of feeling and imagination that encourages the self to turn towards the other in a neighbourly act. Badiou (2003) works with this theological dynamic when referring to Abrahamic and Pauline *universalism* which contests neoliberal capitalism, atomistic individualism and its cultural expression in postmodernism. Badiou's universalism is germane to the Judaeo-Christian ethic which is scandalous because it proclaims a new humanity where socially constructed binaries have been transcended (Galatians 3v28). This ruptures the operations of the principalities and powers of every age, including its manifestation in exchange relations that were reinforced after the economic catastrophe of 2007/08 as the indisputable basis of human organisation. Badiou states that Paul was an attractive 'visionary militant' of the universal which endorses egalitarian ethics (2003: 95 and 104). In fact, 'The production of equality and the casting off, in thought, of differences are the material signs of the universal' (2003: 109). This resonates with the doctrine of *personalism* to which a number of theistic and a-theistic thinkers have contributed. David Jenkins (2002), another former Bishop of Durham during the 1980s, believes that Christianity is a profound expression of personal religion as God is personal (not literally a person) which in theological-speak means that people ultimately matter in what is believed to be a personal and meaningful universe. Of course, this is a statement of faith not verifiable scientific knowledge. The universe is more personal than impersonal because God is personal and was manifested in a person (Robinson, 1973), and works through persons to restructure human existence.

DOI: 10.1057/9781137468468.0005

Personalism

The doctrine of personalism establishes personal relationships as the unconditional principle of anthropological existence. It constitutes a doctrinal corrective to Küng's (1977: 585) existential worry about the overly organised, regulated, bureaucratic, computerised and therefore impersonal nature of existence. Similarly, a decade later, Stone (1987: 198) apocalyptically judged the world to be on a knife-edge between technical rationality and emotional intelligence. We are obsessively busy selecting the conditions of existence to advance technocratic, impersonal and scientific efficiencies that leave 'no place for the emotions, including the finer ones of love and compassion'. Additionally, Meštrović (1997) introduces the sociological concept of post-emotionalism, a condition of existence that exposes the shortcomings of postmodern atomistic individualism, the post-social and post-political. Accordingly, personalism is the necessary corrective to the mixed blessings of scientific and technological advances, the accoutrements of the computer age and the dead-hand of bureaucratic structures, exhorting that relationships between people have ultimate value as Kantian ends not means and should always take priority over the forces of impersonalism. Personalism had doctrinal authority within the personal social services, including the criminal justice system (see my extended discussion, 2010, Chapter 3), but has assumed the unenviable distinction of being relegated to the pre-modern passé, associated with the political iconoclasm of New Labour as we shall see later.

Personalist ethics has produced a number of illustrious academic devotees who can be recounted briefly. Berdyaev's (1935) personalist philosophy endorsed a commitment to the intrinsic worth of human beings that found support in Mounier (1952), resonating with a Kantian morality of ends over means. According to Copleston's exegesis, Mounier's ethic had its roots in the spiritualist tradition of French philosophy which formulated a reaction to those 'intellectual and social–political tendencies which appear to treat man simply as an object of scientific study or to reduce him to his function in the economic sphere or in the social–political totality' (Copleston, 1975/2003: 310). According to Mounier, personalism has similarities to existentialism in its reaction to the Hegelian metaphysical system and world-process that relegates the individual to a fleeting moment in the history of the unfolding Absolute. In other words, Mounier rejects all systems of thought and practices that threaten

DOI: 10.1057/9781137468468.0005

humanity. Buber's (1970) intimate language of I–Thou expresses holistic engagement between the self and other, in opposition to I–object–thing relations. Buber writes of existence as a personal encounter with others, dialogic engagement between two separate beings who meet under conditions of mutuality, reciprocity and equality. Finally, Levinas (see Hand, 1989: 1) refers to face-to-face relations as an 'ethical relation that forever precedes and exceeds the egoism and tyranny of ontology'. Eagleton (2009: 226) acknowledges the harm done by capitalist forces and relations, as well as postmodern culture, which have combined to erode socio-ethical relations at the hands of a bland post-politics replete with instrumental reason and efficiency. This is anathema to Berdyaev, Mounier, Buber and Levinas. For these thinkers 'Ethics is what hurts' (Eagleton, 2009: 235), because of its stringent claims, demands and costs. Let's develop the discussion by stepping into the rarefied atmosphere of Continental Philosophy with Lacan and Žižek.

Psychoanalysis and Symbolic ethics

The primary concern confronting us, germane to theorising the moral, is how to co-exist without gouging lumps off each other. This problematic can be traced through the scientific evidence on the evolution of *Homo sapiens* from earlier human types 200,000 years ago (Harari, 2014). Initially, our ancestors existed in small bands of hunter gatherers who were engaged in the daily struggle for shelter, food and basic survival. Nevertheless, it was the existential conditions imposed by the Agricultural Revolution, 12,000 years ago, that our struggles as a species really began. The perennial growth of crops made it possible to sustain larger populations in towns and cities. Now how are we going to live together? It is theorised that our biological–genetic endowment from hunter gatherers did not conduce to harmonious cooperation which might explain the absence of moral economy. As Harari comments a 'handful of millennia separating the Agricultural Revolution from the appearance of cities, kingdoms and empires was not enough time to allow an instinct of mass cooperation to evolve' (2014: 102 – the chemistry of the brain, physics, biology and genetics raise important questions pertinent to theorising the moral). As we have seen, the intellectual exploration of ethico-cultural co-existence can be traced to the polis of Classical antiquity that constituted a resource for Pauline

DOI: 10.1057/9781137468468.0005

political theology, proceeding through the centuries to the Renaissance and Enlightenment and beyond. It finds contemporary expression in the notion of the *Big Society*. Notwithstanding conceptual ambiguity and the considerable strain placed upon it, the Big Society acknowledges the importance of people coming together, strengthening communities and helping one another (HM Government, 2010a). This resonates with Schweitzer's ethic of reverence for life, Judaeo-Christian and Pauline ethics, Bonhoeffer's ethic of responsibility for others and personalist face-to-face relations.

The reason for tarrying with a psychoanalytical perspective, in the company of Lacan and Žižek, is that it stitches together the formation of human subjectivity (who do we think we are?), ethico-cultural and social conditions, theology and radical politics, which offer additional resources to analyse intellectual and moral transformations pertinent to the criminal justice domain. A suitable point of entry to what is a demanding body of thought is *Rethinking Social Exclusion* (Winlow and Hall, 2013; Elliott, 2005) where attention is directed towards the nature and content of the social, specifically the complex association between individual identity (the *Imaginary*), and the prevailing dominant capitalist order (the *Real*). Winlow and Hall suggest that it is too reductionist to attach the term social exclusion to, for example, the poor or offenders, which conjures up definable subgroups split off from the rest of us who experience the comforts of the social. Rather, neoliberal capitalism and its concomitant postmodern culture has penetrated so deeply into our bones that *all of us* are being excluded from the social by the coercive imposition of a political economy that inculcates the subject with a dystopian state of nature exulting in egoistic self-interest that damages the public interest. This is the disturbing dark night of the world (Sinnerbrink, 2008), not the promotion of intersubjective social relations and dialogic engagement. Whilst Lacan expatiates on the three orders of the human psyche through the categories of the *Imaginary, Symbolic, Real*, it is the Symbolic order which is most pertinent. Roudinesco (2014) clarifies that the Imaginary, Symbolic and Real are the three elements in Lacan's psychic topography.[5]

Although the Imaginary poses an acute problem under neoliberal capitalism because of the promotion of narcissistic obsessions, the release of libidinal energies and dominant material signifiers (see Myers, 2003; also Homer, 2005), by contrast, the Symbolic is the social domain we enter when taking the step from self to other. It can be described as the locus where we play our part in the wider community of fellow human beings, a significant challenge since the Agricultural Revolution. The Symbolic is constituted by language which self-evidently appertains to the social dimension of existence. It is the sphere of social relations and dialogic engagement; rules and regulations; the law of prohibition to prevent actions that cause injury to others. Furthermore, the Symbolic contains the verbal and non-verbal conventions of daily encounters, socially constructed customs and practices, normative codes of conduct and unwritten rules that comprise the expectations we place on each other without which social relations would be problematic. Just as a word is comprised of a combination of letters or marks on a page that acquire meaning in its usage by its precise location in a sentence so, by extrapolation, the individual human subject acquires meaning and value through having and playing a role in the socio-Symbolic order. We must make the transition from self to other, ego to social, state of nature to state of culture, to become a person alongside other persons. Eagleton (2009: 6) clarifies that Lacan derived his thought from Hegel for whom 'the transition from one state to another has an ethical dimension'. Furthermore, Winlow and Hall insightfully explain that it is the 'passage from the "state of nature" to the "state of culture" that Žižek positions subjectivity. For him, subjectivity remains forever tied to the sense of loss and profound negativity that defines the transition. Once we arrive in a "state of culture" we are presented with the substance we can use to "fill up the void of subjectivity"' (2013: 153). By contrast the Real, as the pre-Symbolic, is for Žižek associated with capitalism and postmodernism which has wreaked havoc on the Symbolic, ethico-cultural conditions, moral and social regulation.

The Symbolic (the *Big Other* is Lacan's term for the Symbolic) has a mythical status because it does not intrinsically belong to the ontological furniture of the world. There is no objective or verifiable reality outside of us, and it is not given with or constitutes a permanent fixture of existence (just like Küng's God). However, caution is required when resorting to the language of *myth* to avoid negative associations with fictional untruths. Robinson (1973: 20) suggests that myth has a positive function in connecting *Homo sapiens* to the psychic depths of human experience, and Armstrong (2006) suggests that we create myth as a means of coping with the human condition. In Platonic usage myth is an account of something which is not taken as seriously or with the same level of exactitude as scientific statements (*Phaedo*). Theologically, the Genesis

DOI: 10.1057/9781137468468.0005

myth purports to describe the origins of existence which is different to the account in Harari (2014). But the Genesis account is not supposed to be understood as history, science or literal truth. Rather, its existential function is to articulate a life-view that it is foundationally meaningful and worthwhile (faith not science). Harari (2014: 133) proceeds with the thesis that human beings may not have the requisite biological instincts to establish and sustain 'mass cooperation networks'. To compensate for species biological deficiencies we create myth, imagined orders and cognitive scripts, to facilitate mutual coexistence and call it culture. Nevertheless, one is summoned to invest belief in and commit to it *as if* it were true (again like Küng's *God*) even though we 'know' it does not materially 'exist'. The Symbolically mythological is also ideological: 'Ideology congeals in our neurological circuits and structures consciousness, fashioning the way we think and feel about our world and our place within it' (Winlow and Hall, 2013: 154). But there are an abundance of ideologies in the market place of ideas that invite us to formulate a judgement, and make a decision, about which one we invest with commitment and truth. It is a choice between life and death.

Žižek's response to the existential burdens imposed by capitalism and postmodernism, informed by Hegel's dialectical methodology, Marx's analytical tools and Lacan's psychoanalytical terminology that is transposed into a political register, is a political act to construct a new Symbolic order. This response is also informed by Pauline political theology and the Judaeo-Christian ethic that joins forces with Marxism to construct a new politics to create a new subject in a new world order (Milbank et al, 2010). It has been claimed that the 'New Testament is among other things a polemic against accountancy. Love disrupts the precisely calibrated equivalences of the symbolic order with its carnivalesque refusal to calculate, reckon the cost, return like for like' (Eagleton, 2009: 120). In other words, there are other and better ways of organising the world and human relations, endorsed by the epistolary injunction: 'Do not model yourselves on the behaviour of the world around you, but let your behaviour change, modelled by your new mind' (Romans 12.2). To return to an earlier point, Pauline political theology (Milbank, 2010) did not propose to abolish the biopolitical order of the Roman Empire under the Caesars (Blumenfeld, 2001), but to exist alongside and potentially transform it by incursions of equality, goodness, agapē, justice and truth. For Žižek (2008) the Judaeo-Christian ethic, Pauline theology and universalism, constitute a radical alternative to the capitalist order

DOI: 10.1057/9781137468468.0005

and the subjectivity it fashions. Accordingly, 'Žižek's writing, stranded somewhere between high modernism and postmodern pastiche, can be viewed as an attempt to develop a psychosocial diagnosis of the self in its dealings with the global capitalist economy' (Harrington, 2005: 184). In doing so it constructs a set of intellectual and ethical coordinates by which to analyse our present condition and steer a course out of it, out of an absurd present and into an open future for which we alone are responsible and which can be different to current arrangements. Žižek, establishing the role of atheistic theologian, states, 'I think this is the legacy of Christianity – this legacy of God not as a big Other or guarantee but God as the ultimate ethical agency who puts the burden on us to organize ourselves' (2010: 180). This is Badiou's universalism and Bonhoeffer's ethic of responsibility in contradistinction to capitalist arrangements and postmodern culture.

To anticipate a later discussion, it can be suggested at this juncture that probation's historical lineage and cultural traditions, forged in the period of *penal–welfare* and personal social services, its reformist ideology and discrete but essential role in the dialectics of criminal justice, have been eroded by relegation into a state of nature, the capitalist Real. This transformation, underway since the 1980s, has dislodged the cultural symbols, historical artifacts, inherited ways of thinking and operating, recognisable meanings and personalist values. The circuits of ethico-cultural contestation, of rehabilitation and welfare, have been destabilised by privatisation and marketisation that, in Žižek's language, is the transposition from the Symbolic into the Real, from a moral economy to capitalist political economy. For organisational staff it has become the terrifying dark night of the world, of which Payment by Results is the material signifier of the re-energised capitalist dispensation after 2007/08 (Whitehead, 2015). The symbolic efficiency of probation comprised a set of discernible values that congealed into organisational circuits, reproduced by training, staff supervision, the cultural transmission of organisational know-how and the maintenance of professional standards (Whitehead and Thompson, 2004). The tensions and sometimes conflicts generated by probation, questions posed, the mediating checks and balances, in pursuit of criminal and social justice, were first eroded then seriously undermined as Chapters 3 and 4 will recount. The situation in probation was never perfect (Box, 1987), there never was a 'Golden Age' (Statham, 2014), but it was intellectually and morally different compared to those conditions released since the 1980s. But first,

DOI: 10.1057/9781137468468.0005

from assembling some of the intellectual resources to theorise the moral, I need to address specific references to moral economy which begin to narrow the focus of this enquiry.

Politico-economic and moral conditions before and after the great transformation

Human beings have never operated, nor has their subjectivity been fashioned, within a fully functioning moral economy of people before profit, the public interest before self-interest. There is too much historical and contemporary evidence of violent competition, power struggles, ideological clashes, trade routes and markets, imperialist adventures and empire building that prized material advancement more than the attractions of moral economy (Bobbitt, 2002). Although 19th century liberal capitalism was politically, socially, and economically *different* in degree to conditions that appertained prior to industrialisation, such differences should not be over-stated. Hall (2012) alludes to merchant adventurers operating 1000 years ago, and the Venetian Empire between the 12th and 16th centuries carved out trade routes lubricated by fiscal calculation, commodities, business enterprises and ruthless competition. During these centuries Venice functioned as a precursor of the capitalist system (Arrighi, 2010) propelled forward by the Dutch in the 18th century, London in the 19th century with investment capital accrued from the slave trade, then the United States in the 20th century. Venice was the strategic geo-political hub of an extensive trading empire throughout the Adriatic, reaching beyond Constantinople into the markets of the Black Sea and the Eastern Mediterranean. Almost everything was up for sale in a profit-driven trading empire that stimulated desire over need and where culture followed economics. The principal commercial centre was the Rialto, the island location for the first settlers seeking sanctuary from the Germanic incursions into the Italian mainland sixteen hundred years ago. We can extend the historical lineage even further to Kiberd's (2009: 280) delightful text on Joyce's *Ulysses*, in which the Homeric Odysseus is 'treated often as a travelling salesman or barterer, and he is even taunted for being a profiteering merchant rather than an aristocratic athlete'. Capitalism did not suddenly erupt *ex nihilo* in the 19th century fully formed, as there were previous archaeological deposits that signposted future expansion.

DOI: 10.1057/9781137468468.0005

The same analytical caution is required when excavating the concept of moral economy. Tönnies (2002) differentiated between gemeinschaft and gesellschaft; Weber (1968) between substantive and instrumental social action; and Durkheim (1984) mechanical compared to organic solidarity. Furthermore, the aforementioned Augustine–Aquinas theological world-view collapsed under the weight of Enlightenment modernity. These differentially recounted transformations can be evaluated, critiqued, even lamented, but they do not constitute a decisive historical fracture between a previously functioning moral economy and its subsequent displacement by the inexplicable capitalist Real. It is possible to glean evidence from the annals of antiquity to speculate that human beings have exercised moral sensibility in various historical epochs. For example, the Judaeo-Christian ethic was a *counterfactual absurdity* to the principalities and powers of the Roman Empire. There were codes of chivalry during the Middle Ages and ecclesiastical influences mediated knightly behaviour (Burrow, 2009). Hastings (2013: 539) recounts the parlous situation towards the end of 1914, several months into the First World War. Although war threatens to destroy what is often only a veneer of moral convention, it was nevertheless possible for some combatants to maintain their moral scruples *in extremis*. But these illustrations do not provide the evidence of a moral economy that integrated individual citizens into a symbolic order of mutuality, reciprocity and intersubjectivity. It is reasonable to assume that during former centuries, as now, some homo sapiens more than others exercised the capacity of reason to deduce appropriate moral responses; were dutiful; acquired and exercised moral sensitivity; were psychologically predisposed to sociability consolidated by socialisation that inculcated personalist values and humane responses towards others, rather than Hobbesian self-interest and the infliction of harm. These matters are as complex as they are contested and the evidence appertaining to political conditions, economic arrangements and traces of moral economy pose their own problems of historical interpretation. With these qualifications in mind I want to explore some of the evidence on moral economy in the extant literature.

If one of the connecting threads of morality adumbrated in this chapter is a capacity to transcend self-interest, it has been argued that economic arrangements in pre-market societies were embedded within ethico-cultural relations described as moral economy. In other words, economic forces and relations were not detached from family and community relations. There was closer socio-Symbolic and moral integration compared to the disembedded arrangements that occurred in the 19th century that fostered atomistic individualism in a system of exploitative exchange relations (Sayer, 2000). Booth (1994; see also Block, 2006) covers similar ground when theorising moral economy, suggesting that pre-capitalist market economies were embedded in social relations in which economic forces were mediated by non-economic forces of family, social and communal relations. Booth says that 'before modernity, the securing of human livelihood had no separateness – no boundary line that marked it out as distinct from the enveloping society's institutions and values' (1994: 653). This adds evidential weight to the position that pre-market economic arrangements were located within, and structured by, ethico-cultural phenomena that regulated market exchange. Harari (2014: 356) suggests that before the Industrial Revolution daily life for most human beings operated within the three interlocking circuits of family, extended family and local community. It was the nuclear family that was primarily responsible for the cognitive and emotional well-being of its members, and their health requirements. This was not a moral economy but, more accurately, a difference in conditions of life compared to the future capitalist political economy. Fundamentally, this difference was between family and community, state and market, carved out by the *great transformation*[6] (Polanyi, 2001). In a market economy, now increasingly market society (Sandel, 2012), the economic system breaks free from the circuits of ethico-cultural regulation which is anathema to Schweitzer, Küng, Bonhoeffer, Judaeo-Christian and personalist ethics, precisely because of the symbolic damage inflicted on human beings by the decline in symbolic efficiency (the Big Other).

E.P. Thompson (1971) evaluates the transition from pre-market to laissez faire economic arrangements during the 18th and 19th centuries. He marshalls numerous items of evidence to argue that the paternalistic model of the manufacturing and marketing process which facilitated the flow of goods direct from the farmer or cottage industry to the customer was slowly breaking down. The paternalistic model which accommodated 'at least some symbolic solidarity between the rulers and the poor' (1971: 129) gave way to a different set of political, economic, social and moral arrangements between rulers, ruled and the operation of capital. Although political, economic and social arrangements in the 17th and 18th centuries, and previously, were assuredly complex, 'The new economy (of liberal capitalism) entailed a de-moralizing of the theory of trade and consumption' (1971: 89). In other words, it had been unnatural that anyone would profit and achieve an advantage at the expense of others. In pre-capitalist societies the notion of a fair price for goods and services was more important than a free market price, and that peasants could express disapproval to large farmers who sold surpluses at a higher price outside the locale of the village, at the expense of the basic needs of those in the village. Tellingly, 'The breakthrough of the new political economy of the free market was also the breakdown of the old moral economy of provision' (1971: 136). Scott (1976) suggests that pre-capitalist societies were different to modern capitalist societies in the sense that they put safety and reliability over profit and exchange relations.[7]

Dyer (2000) digs deeper into these matters in his excavations of the Middle Ages, specifically the people of Britain between 850 and 1520. He, too, makes the point that this period was different to what emerged after the 1780s. Nevertheless, the earlier period was decidedly complex as there were cyclical economic changes, in addition to continuities on either side of the *great transformation* divide. Evidence is advanced to support the view that peasants produced to sustain themselves *and* for the market place. There was also predatory profiteering and that between 1100 and 1315 the 'rise in population and commercial activity threatened to weaken the community' (2000: 183). This is hardly an endorsement for moral economy. Dyer sketches a complex and ambivalent socioeconomic and moral situation in which harvest conventions made provision for the poor and individual initiative was prized, but 'the peasants who shared these entrepreneurial and selfish tendencies were still contained within highly cohesive communities' (2000: 185). There were smaller units of production in crafts, people working from home, family workplaces and farms, local trade in goods and services. Thomas (2009) covers a similar historical period but asserts that 'political and religious principles were a matter of bitter dispute, and rural society was riven by feuds and petty hostilities. The harmony of the local community was always precarious and often non-existent' (2009: 189). Then, as now, the active pursuit of self-interest and personal gain could be seen as an exemplar of personal initiative and a responsible moral act. This view has a distinguished pedigree that should be considered in more detail as we travel towards the end of the first chapter.[8]

Adam Smith 1723–90 (1759/2009 and 1776) was writing on the cusp of the *great transformation* towards capitalism whose *invisible hand* would ensure that self-interest benefitted others. This economic maxim

DOI: 10.1057/9781137468468.0005

offered a deliciously constructed but convoluted justification for self-promotion. In other words, get on with the business of making a profit according to the laws of *Market Whys and Wherefores* (Jenkins, 2004: 4349), and the public good will take care of itself. Jenkins is insightful because he contextualises Smith's economics within early Enlightenment thought with its ideology of the harmony of nature guaranteed by the divine (deistic) presence. In a providential world of regular and divinely ordained Newtonian mathematical patterns that function like clockwork, the pursuit of individual self-interest contributed to the functioning of the harmonious whole – very neat. However, this thesis requires qualification by acknowledging that the *Wealth of Nations* (the 1776 economic book) was written after the *Theory of Moral Sentiments* (the 1759 moral philosophy book). Human beings may well engage in self-interested pursuits but they are capable of, indeed interested in, the happiness of others. In fact, imagination and sympathy are necessary conditions for justice and benevolence. Accordingly, money and fame should be kept in perspective; exercise prudence (take care of yourself); do justice (do not hurt others); and exercise public-spirited beneficence (be good to others). These qualities combine to make the world a better place. What Smith could not foresee were the monstrous effects of laissez faire liberal capitalism during the 19th century, how economic interest would swamp moral sentiment and that the *invisible hand* would malfunction as self-interest does not necessarily produce beneficial socio-moral effects. Accordingly, the progression of liberal capitalism, following the *great transformation*, is not a civilisation but a pseudo-pacification process (Hall, 2012). Not a reduction of aggressive libidinal drives through the intervention of Enlightenment reason, but rather conversion into a sublimated form. The cult of exchange relations, fearful competition, the glorification of profit, have hollowed out the reproductive circuits of ethico-cultural values and any hope of a moral economy through the destructive release of harmful forces and relations. Outram argues that the 18th century 'opened up enormous moral and intellectual problems that did not become easier to solve once they were projected onto a world stage' (2013: 72). Nineteenth century liberalism is now the neoliberal order. As we shall see below, under the guise of opening up the criminal justice system to the public, private and voluntary sectors, stimulating competition to enhance performance through the Rehabilitation Revolution, the release of market energies has damaged the circuits of ethico-cultural contestation. This is condensed in the material signifier

DOI: 10.1057/9781137468468.0005

of Payment by Results, contingent on the demise of probation, which represents the rejection of the system's reproductive moral core.

Next, Hegel (1770–1831) was Smith's (1723–90) contemporary for 20 years. Hegel was sensitive to the social and spiritual predicament of modernity, but at first sight cuts it both ways at once. He exults in individual freedom, self-interest and Enlightenment rationality within Smith's emerging market society, whilst recognising the threat of freedom to the *Ethical Life*. Egoism constitutes a threat but this is not always negative, especially if the individual finds fulfillment through the performance of social roles – the family, social institutions, civil society and the state. You have the right to freedom and the pursuit of self-interest as a rational human being, but taken to extremes can damage socio-ethical relations. Accordingly, the ideal condition is the reconciliation of the particular and universal, self-interest with the common interest. Terry Pinkard's (2000) intellectual biography elucidates that Hegel was aware that extremes of poverty and wealth damage social solidarity (see Piketty, 2014; Wilkinson and Pickett, 2009 make the same point supported by empirical evidence). Such extremes damage social solidarity for 'the poor because they have no stake in it, the rich because they tend to think that they can buy themselves out of its obligations' (Pinkard, 2000: 486). Therefore, the State has a duty to correct imbalances and social institutions are required to foster the bonds of social cohesion. An unregulated economy, a malfunctioning division of labour and the production of atomistic individualism, pose threats to social life and universal human interests (Durkheim, 1984). Hegel's concern with unrestrained freedom and unregulated markets anticipated Keynesianism a century later (see discussion in Plant, 1973; and Cullen, 1979) and Eagleton comments (2009: 125), when reflecting on Hegel, social relations can be conceived as the fusion on the Imaginary and Symbolic. Finally, when discussing the perils of extremes we should return to the chapter's starting point of classical ethics.

As with Paul earlier, so too Aristotle, the domain of ethics is also the domain of politics which address the fundamentals of what is good, fair and right. Aristotle's *Ethics* (2000) is a teleological treatise concerned with human actions conducive to what is good. The progression in Aristotle's reasoning begins with the concept of the good, and the most perfect good is not instrumental to any other good, but good in itself which is *eudaimonia* – translated as happiness, behaving well, faring well. Copleston summarises: 'But if there is an end which we desire for

DOI: 10.1057/9781137468468.0005

its own sake and for the sake of which we desire all other subordinate ends or goals, then this ultimate good will be the best good, in fact, *the* good' (1946/2003: 332). The good that produces happiness is not a matter of mathematical computation, scientific equation or economic calculation, but human judgement. Next, the good person lives according to the virtues or human excellences. The intellectual virtues are wisdom, intelligence and prudence; the moral virtues are liberality and temperance. Virtue, says Aristotle, is the *mean* between excess and deficiency. For example, the mean between rashness and cowardice is courage. I will argue later that developments in the criminal justice system in general, precisely because of what has happened to probation in particular, can be reframed as the collapse of the intellectual and moral virtues. The politics of coercive imposition through seising command and control for political more than penological reasons has shunted the criminal justice system away from the mean towards excess, from the Symbolic towards the Real. This is evidenced by the decline of probation mediation, its checks and balances and the escalation of retributive punishment and prison. Furthermore, the story recounted in Chapter 3 and 4 will advance the argument that criminal justice, specifically since 1992, has taken leave of its capacity for rational thought and emotional sensibility, contingent upon the collapse of intellectual and moral virtues. This is a consequence of coercive impositions from without rather than evolution from within. If, for Plato (1974), there is a transcendental foundation to the content of the moral law, Aristotle brings us down to earth by emphasising immanence. It is more practical reason than metaphysical reason, a life-view for the polis rather than a world-view, which returns us to the point where we commenced this chapter in the company of Schweitzer. Not so much a question of metaphysics but aesthetics – goodness, fairness, justice as aesthetically pleasing qualities among human beings. Accordingly, 'Aristotle's treatment of the moral virtues is often enlightening and shows his common-sense moderation and clear judgement' (Copleston, 1946/2003: 340).

As I arrive at the end of this chapter which has assembled some of the intellectual resources to theorise the moral, its content and aetiology, the fault line exposed since the Age of Reason and Industrial Revolution is that of the particular–universal, self–other, ego–benevolence. The condition of modernity promoted Marxist alienation and Durkheimian anomie. Fenton, commenting on the Durkheimian corpus, stated that 'Social life without moral regulation is a monstrosity, it is a descent into

DOI: 10.1057/9781137468468.0005

anarchy, it is a denial of all that is elementally true of society. Moral regulation is simultaneously necessary to the health of the social order and health of the individual' (1984: 85). Contrastingly, Weber the 'ardent German nationalist and free market liberal' (Allen, 2004: 5) who, along with Adam Smith (but with qualifications) and more contemporary exponents including Hayek and Friedman, line themselves up behind self-interest as the main driver of economic and social progress. I have exposed other fault lines pertinent to the discussion in this chapter:

Kant v. Bentham
Deontology v. utility
Motives v. consequences
Substantive rationality v. instrumental rationality
Atomistic individualism v. universalism
Self v. public interest
Qualitative service outputs v. quantitative numerical outcomes
Personal Social Services and welfare as end in themselves v.
    calculation, 3Es, VfM
Keynes v. neoliberal capitalism
Political economy v. moral economy

Systems of morality, the claim of ethics (MacIntyre, 1967), the concept of moral economy introduced earlier no more belong, intrinsically, to the ontological structure of the world than politico-economic systems. These phenomena are not *given* with or naturally woven into the texture of existence as immutable points of physiocratic reference. Even if they were, they would not be accessible to empirical verification because of deficiencies within our epistemological equipment. Socrates taught us that human beings claim to know more than it is possible to know. Additionally, once we have decided upon an ethico-cultural way of life or established a politico-economic system by which to organise human affairs – whether that is reverence for life, Enlightenment reason, liberal capitalism or Keynesian social democracy – they are always susceptible to disturbance, erosion or even replacement, sometimes with far reaching consequences for the course of human existence. Morality is a matter of practical reason, that is, reason with a practical moral function involving judgement and choice, not abstract theoretical reason. It necessitates an existential decision on how we want to live, conduct our relationships, the content of our cognitive–emotional engagement with others, the meanings and values we consider worth prioritising,

DOI: 10.1057/9781137468468.0005

including politico-economic structures and supporting social organisations. None of these appurtenances are given, permanently fixed, historically determined, spontaneous forces of nature or even uncontested. Each new generation must reformulate its judgements and decisions about the present and future organisation of human life. This applies as much to political economy as criminal justice. At this point we need to turn specifically to the concept of moral economy before putting it to work in the criminal justice system.

Notes

1   Volumes of autobiography: Schweitzer 1955; 1962; also, Parts 1 and 2 of the *Philosophy of Civilization*, 1961 and 1929. There is a copious secondary literature: Seaver, 1947; Mozley, 1950; and Russell, 1941. There is also an informative documentary on Schweitzer's life and work at www.youtube.com/watch?v=Gf4B9vosoCY.

2   In the Preface (1929), Schweitzer asserts that the content and meaning of ethics is *reverence for life*. The good 'consists in maintaining, promoting, and enhancing life and that destroying, injuring, and limiting life are evil' (xiv). He subjects numerous ethical systems to the criterion of reverence for life beginning with Socrates, Plato, Aristotle and other contributions from the classical world. He alludes to religious and philosophical world views; the pre- and post-Renaissance period of Hartley, Hobbes, Locke, Bentham, Smith, Hutcheson and Shaftesbury; the Enlightenment with Kant, Hegel, Schopenhauer and Nietzsche. Ethical systems are exposed to rigorous critique before expatiating on reverence for life, its civilizing power and mission.

3   This is a significant statement on Pauline metaphysics and political ethics: 'Paul engages in political metaphysics. It is because dikaiosunē is the essence of God and of God's office that the world is possible, that a universal society can be built and can endure ... If in Plato dikaiosunē (δικαιοσύνη) makes the individual one and the polis possible, in Paul dikaiosunē makes humanity equal and the whole world one, a metaphysical but also a political understanding' (Blumenfeld, 2001: 416).

4   Some primary texts: Bonhoeffer 1963; 1955; 1966; and 1971. Secondary texts: Bethge (1970); Dumas (1971); Metaxas (2010) whose text complements the documentary drama *Agent of Grace* at: www.youtube.com/watch?v=bj9jMSs5fQg.

5   The *Imaginary* refers to the order during the early stage of human development, the formation of the self, identity, ego and consciousness. For Lacan it is a psychic space of self-estrangement, redolent of how the ego

fixes upon some feature of the external world by which it is seduced and manipulated (material status, consumer culture). The Imaginary is a complex hidden space where it is not 'apparent whether I am myself or another, inside or outside myself, behind or before the mirror' (Eagleton, 2009: 3). The *Symbolic* order is 'outside' the self, yet to which the self is related and ordered. It is the locus of social institutions, customs, laws and prohibitions, into which individuals are socialised, or not. Human subjectivity is the product of the Symbolic. The *Real* is the pre-symbolic, the source of the unexplained, in-articulated and drives. It is beyond language. For a detailed exposition of these three Lacanian psychic orders, see Lacan (2001); Winlow and Hall (2013); Žižek (1992; 2006).

6   The thesis that 19th century industrial capitalism, its market transformations, did not occur by accident, nor by an unstoppable force of nature or spontaneous occurrence. Rather, it was driven forward by the state, pulling up the past to embed laissez faire to re-mould society. Capitalist political economy, like moral economy, is a human artefact. See Marquand: 'Today's markets are constituted by states, sustained by states, regulated by states, protected by states and sometimes imposed by states' (2014: 81).

7   Heptonstall, formerly situated in the West Riding of Yorkshire, was a location for handloom weaving in the Middle Ages prior to the *great transformation* of mechanisation and large-scale industrialisation of the wool trade. Handloom weavers worked from home in small scale family cottage industries to produce wool products. Towards the end of the 18th century the finished cloths were taken to the Piece Hall in Halifax, approximately 8 miles away, to be sold to merchants. However, the industrial revolution, expansion of new technologies and development of large-scale factory enterprises culminated in the decline of Heptonstall and rise of Hebden Bridge in the Calder valley below. The author visited these three locations during the weekend of 8–10 June 2012.

8   For a contemporary discussion of moral economy see Wiegratz (2010; 2011). Wiegratz says that neoliberal reforms in Uganda have reshaped material, social and cultural conditions. Pre-neoliberal norms and values have been displaced with those of a market society. The material and ideological foundations of neoliberalism have restructured normative moral conditions, from the circuits of moral economy to a marketised political economy and its implications for human relations.

DOI: 10.1057/9781137468468.0005

2
Moral Economy: Exploring a Contested Concept

Abstract: *The intellectual resources on morality assembled in the previous chapter contribute to and facilitate the task of refining the conceptual device of moral economy. Accordingly, I now proceed from a preparatory discussion on the subject of morality, to the specifics of moral economy. It is urgent and vital to advance thinking on the content of, arguments for, the mode of conceptualisation and articulation of what is a contested concept. I also begin to weave moral economy with criminal justice and probation.*

Whitehead, Philip. *Reconceptualising the Moral Economy of Criminal Justice: A New Perspective.* Basingstoke: Palgrave Macmillan, 2015. DOI: 10.1057/9781137468468.0006.

DOI: 10.1057/9781137468468.0006

From intellectual resources to the specifics of moral economy

The previous chapter assembled some of the multilayered intellectual resources to excavate the concept of the moral. This enquiry was funnelled to explore pertinent references to moral economy in the literature and the nature of its existence before and after the *great transformation*. The next step narrows the focus further by confirming that ethics is the philosophical study of moral questions, and the term ethics and morality have been used interchangeably in the previous chapter. Moral philosophers have reflected on the telos (τελός end) of morality, an exemplar being the aforementioned good life in Aristotle's (2000) *Nicomachean Ethics*. Additionally, ethical systems address intrinsic worth and value. Arguably, neoliberal capitalism constitutes a politico-economic *and* ethical system concerned with the *end* of human existence. Here, the good life is premised upon the pursuit of personal gain from which everyone in the polis (πόλις) benefits as material wealth trickles down. The doctrinal creed is that greed, egoistically pursued, is so good that it results in beneficence for all. The verifiable and experiential flaw with this model is that how capitalism is supposed to work is not, in fact, how it does work. The evidence from Piketty's (2014) monumental edifice that draws on extensive historical and comparative data sources on capitalist organisation is that it demonstrably sucks up wealth more than it cascades down, and self-interest is self-evidently not converted into benevolence. Let us not be churlish and give credit where it's due by acknowledging its exemplary capacity to create material wealth, but the system cannot guarantee that wealth is acquired fairly or distributed equitably. Material benefits come at the expense of socioeconomic inequality that inflicts damage on all of us (Wilkinson and Pickett, 2009). The material surface that shimmers with its tantalising promise of fiscal bliss masks an underbelly of disturbing unethical outcomes. I refer to capitalist organisation to make the case that it is conceptually, materially and ethically *different* to the substance of moral economy, my primary concern. Marquand (2014) has a different take on the matter, which I dispute, because he employs the concept in looser fashion to argue that British history, over the last 200 years, has manifested four different moral economies. First, the period before the great transformation when moral economy was the ideological property of the crowd (Thompson, 1971); second, 19th century laissez faire liberal capitalism; third, Keynesian social democracy that

DOI: 10.1057/9781137468468.0006

established the social-welfare state from 1945 until the late-1970s; finally, the neoliberal era since the 1980s that constitutes the historical parameter for the re-framing of criminal justice in Chapters 3 and 4.

This is not my usage because the operational circuits of capital accumulation and market expansion compete with the circuits of ethico-cultural contestation to produce different conditions of existence and individual subjectivity. Capitalist exchange relations, the extraction of time and resources from minds and bodies, exploitation, barbaric and violent competition between individuals and nations, are fixed in mortal combat with a moral economy of regard for others, the common welfare, and equality. A system where it is more blessed to receive than to give (exchange relations) is diametrically opposed to a system where it is more blessed to give than receive. Both have their historical progenitors, ends and aspirations, ways of organising and prioritising life in the polis, operating circuits and mechanisms of reproduction that have determinative anthropological and social implications. Capitalist political economy is a class project played out through markets, capital flows, investment opportunities, profit, self-interest and fearful competition, a free for all of un-freedom exemplified by the unequal distribution of material resources and life opportunities. It privatises state assets, liberalises global trade, deregulates financial institutions and labour, and commercialises human life. It is by nature predatory (Galbraith, 2008), taking out more than it puts in. Since its revival in the neoliberal 1980s and paradoxically, but not unexpectedly, the great leap forward after the capitalist tremours of 2007–08, it inflicts social murder (Chernomas and Hudson, 2007) and exacerbates social inequality which is a 'fundamental feature of capitalism generally, [whose] reproduction is part of the logic of this system' (Duménil and Lévy, 2004: 137).

Accordingly, my main concern, informed by the cast of resources in Chapter 1, is to direct attention to the content of, argument for, the mode of conceptualisation and articulation of moral economy. I advance the position that moral economy functions as a conceptual device to forge links with, and put into sharp relief, the probation ideal and rehabilitative ethic in the criminal justice system which have been systematically dismantled through the politics of disavowal over recent decades. It also demonstrates, during the next two chapters, that the period before the 1980s was different to what followed. It is evidentially the case that 'They did things differently then, and thought and felt differently' (Burrow, 2009: 115). The conceptual lens of moral economy folds into the Weberian *ideal type*, a methodological procedure that compensates for

DOI: 10.1057/9781137468468.0006

investigative limitations in the social sciences. If social phenomena are ambiguous and cannot be observed directly, the ideal type is constructed to discover the relevant properties of what is subjected to investigation. Moral economy, as conceptual device or ideal type, accentuates certain features of reality. In other words, it is a caricature related to reality, but not its exact representation. Consequently, it functions as a heuristic device, it is elucidatory, identifies traits, advances comparative analysis and can be put to work to expose intellectual and moral deficiency.

Building content

The concept of moral economy is indubitably complex, contested and ambiguous, but not insignificant. The following sketch may be disposed of as too speculative and theoretically abstract, with little prospect of implementation in the near or distant future. In other words, it is too Platonically metaphysical to be of any Aristotelian earthly good. Nevertheless, it is a concept requiring careful consideration. The starting point for this reconstruction is that the foundational content of moral economy asserts the unconditional value of human existence. Schweitzer's anthropological ethic advanced a life-view where the primary principle of the moral is reverence for life. Its inviolable and personal nature is in and of itself self-sufficiently and self-evidently good. This is the platform upon which to conduct human relations, its sphere of interest encapsulating just and right dealings within the organisation of the polis. It is a life-view with micro (individual subjectivity), mezzo (organisational) and macro (political economy) dimensions. Its content can be further enriched by the Kantian kingdom of ends, not calculable means; Weberian substantive rationality, not instrumental rationality as the motivation for social action; benevolence is valued more highly than egoistic self-interest. This requires a decisive yet difficult move from the self to the other to establish intersubjective social relations of mutuality, empathy and trust. When Schweitzer issued the invitation in the aftermath of the First World War to 'look for a human being or some work devoted to human welfare' (1929: 260), it was not possible for everyone to emulate Bonhoeffer in activating an ethical injunction that sacrificially cost his life. However, social workers, probation officers and others employed in the people-facing professions assimilated this ethical rationality within their respective organisations. Probation work, within the criminal justice system, was an integral component of the

DOI: 10.1057/9781137468468.0006

post-war Keynesian settlement (Skidelsky, 2003) as a public good, delivering a public service, as a public duty, largely to a disadvantaged section of the public. It belonged to the personal social services that operationalised a personalist ethic until, that is, the profession was trashed by the politics of New Public Management and its supporting musculature of managerial consultants. Probation's pioneering mission constructed structural, cultural and biographical analyses of the human condition to understand and explain offending behaviour, an intellectual and moral task on behalf of the state and criminal justice system.

Schweitzer and Bonhoeffer on civilisation and philosophical ethics, Küngian theology and Christology, Pauline epistolary resources appertaining to political ethics, the Judaeo-Christian inheritance, entreaties on personalism and the Symbolic order, assert the ethico-cultural significance of being men and women for others as the definitive norm of responsibility and maturity. This requires a transformed politico-ethical order that eradicates socially constructed binaries. It is committed to agapē (ἀγάπη), a veritable scandal because it represents a radical challenge to the organisation of life immersed in self-interest, extracting from others to advance the self. The content of moral economy is enriched by Badiou's references to Abrahamic and Pauline exemplars where equality constitutes a material sign of the universal. Indubitably all citizens in the polis matter and socially constructed binary distinctions, the extreme differential allocation of material resources, the signs and symbols of material success and status, must be transcended. Transcendence is achieved through commitment to a higher unity that for some is the theologian's God, or Other. For others a Symbolic order, or Big Other, that fashions a subjectivity different to that required by the capitalist system. Moral economy makes demands, requires existential choices, and is sacrificially costly in human resources and time. It functions within the circuits of a value system where it is preferable to give than receive, agapē not exchange relations, where humanity is one and not divided by the cult of narcissistic hyper-individualism. It is in marked contrast to politico-economic and social organisation that favour an elite who acquire a surfeit of power and material resources, wielded over others to maintain and reproduce a competitive advantage. Its symbol is a sacrificial and renunciating cross (σταυρός), not the semiotics of material excess so highly prized by consumer culture and its media outlets. It is dialogic, face-to-face not in your face, and it is as absurd and scandalous as unorthodox. It cuts against the grain by challenging *the way the world*

DOI: 10.1057/9781137468468.0006

is in arguing for justice (δικαιοσύνη), fairness, equality and the virtues of moral excellence and goodness. Moral economy is preoccupied with the requisite content to further the good life in the polis.

James Joyce (see Kiberd, 2009), as literary artist, conveyed the moral vision in Ulysses that public spaces, the streets where people come into contact with each other, teach social relations. During the early 20th century Joyce was aware of much wrongdoing – Dublin subjected to the imperial yoke of the British Empire, the baleful influence of the Roman Catholic Church from birth to death, Irish and Jews as hated peoples, the great weight of history pressing down with force, hatred, racism and bigotry. These were not the components of agapē (ἀγάπη), this was not life, yet 'Growth is possible, even for settled citizens like Bloom, through openness to the Other, a willingness to talk with those who might seem different' (2009: 246). Similarly, for George Eliot in Middlemarch, human relationships are unquestionably complex but if taken seriously they come with the invitation to grow beyond self-centredness: 'If I really care for you – if I try to think myself into your position and orientation – then the world is bettered by my effort at understanding and comprehension' (Mead, 2014: 223 – *the social worker's and probation officer's creed*). Empathy and imaginative understanding attenuate egoism, so that human growth is possible through openness to others, in taking the step from self to other, from the closed world of the ego to intersubjective relations. It is the leap from darkness to light, nature to culture, the fusion of imaginary and symbolic, resonating with the injunction that in order to find oneself one must lose oneself in the *Ethical Life*. Moral economy is doing good not evil, it strengthens the fainthearted, supports the weak, helps the afflicted; it is agapē, service and the capacity for self-sacrifice. Although human beings act from questionable motives, we are nevertheless capable of sympathy, benevolence, and, as Adam Smith deduced, show an interest in the fortune of others (1759/2009: 13). Not to do this is a persistent threat to the stability of the socio-moral order.

To repeat, the concept of moral economy is complex and contested. It is enshrouded in ambiguity and ambivalence, and some might say irrelevance. However, it is not insignificant because, historically and culturally, it informed the work of the criminal justice system through the *probation ideal*. Probation, from its statutory beginnings during the early 20th century, has performed tasks on behalf of the state whilst operating with a measure of organisational independence until, that is, relatively recently. Its rationale, although containing a mélange of competing ideological

DOI: 10.1057/9781137468468.0006

perspectives (see Whitehead, 2010 on various models of practice), exemplified a humane approach to understanding the biological, psychological and sociological correlates of offending behaviour. It was also, at its very best, a humanising influence throughout the whole system. Probation officers responded to Schweitzer's advice to find vocational work to facilitate human welfare through which they could make a difference as well as make a living. They understood something of and practiced reverence for life (towards offenders, victims and local communities), criminal and social justice. They implemented a life-view that blended cognitive insight with empathic sensibility, professional duty to the courts and passion for the job conducted through relationships that combined the professional and personal. Moral economy is not identical to the probation ideal, but functions as a conceptual device to bring into view a moral dimension to probation practice expressed in the terminology of the rehabilitative ethic. So a trinity of overlapping components: an intellectually supportive moral economy; the probation ideal; and rehabilitative ethic (see extended discussion in Whitehead, 2010: 65–81 for these archaeological deposits). The central features of the probation ideal were as follows:

▸ Informed by religious, humanitarian and personalist impulses that combined to humanise the criminal justice system.

▸ Utilised the human sciences, from psychology to criminology and social theory, to excavate the aetiology of complex behavioural patterns. Understanding incorporated both *what* and *why* dimensions (*what* have you done and *why* have you done it?) to explain offending to magistrates and judges by taking account of structural, cultural and biographical variables (Whitehead and Thompson, 2004).

▸ From a Joycean perspective the probation ideal involved openness to the other and a curiosity about behavioural repertoires. It concurred with George Eliot that the world can be a better place by understanding and comprehension, which was the function of the Social Enquiry Report to advance.

▸ The probation ideal supported a constructive and educative approach in the community wherever possible, which symbolised something more positive than punishment and prison. It was part of the personal social work services, not retributive punishment.

▸ Operated with a narrative of tolerance, human decency, caring control and compassion, empathy, support and help which was its vocational public duty.

DOI: 10.1057/9781137468468.0006

▸ Believed that people can change and so did not give up on others. Relationships were at the centre of practice – good and right in themselves, and effective. Maruna (2001) asserted that offenders can be immersed into a new symbolic order through metanoia (μετανοια as a change of heart and mind).

▸ It explicated that probation officers were the social workers of the criminal and civil courts, therefore different to other staff within the organisations of criminal justice.

▸ The probation ideal included intellectual curiosity and moral obligation, qualitative service outputs, deontological ethics, substantive rationality, and the rehabilitative ethic. In other words, probation work and its diverse services could be justified by being good and right in themselves. Probation may not reduce reoffending; it may accomplish 'nothing'. Rather, good for its own sake and operated a good will, which has been relegated to the unmodern. This is the probation ideal, ethical and aesthetic.

Although there are well rehearsed objections to the rehabilitative ethic that reach back to the 1970s,[1] it complemented the probation ideal. But the collapse of the rehabilitative ethic in conjunction with the probation ideal has created an intellectual and moral vacuum in criminal justice (Bottoms and Preston, 1980; Garland, 1985 and 2001). In fact 'The collapse of this model exposes us to the moral debate about the values which should be operative in our criminal justice system' (Wood, 1991: 61 which anticipates Faulkner's letter of 1993 later). This discussion on the content of moral economy that overlaps with the probation ideal and rehabilitative ethic, asserts that the past was unlike the present morally and intellectually, cognitively and emotionally; things were different then. The jewel that used to shine in Kantian fashion has been cast aside and crushed by the politics of disavowal and relegation into the Real (Chapters 3 and 4). When turning from content to argument in support of moral economy, a few general comments to start with.

Supportive arguments

Whether we like it or not – sometimes we don't, hell can be other people, we are attracted to and repulsed by the Nietzschean herd, the neighbour as enemy and competitor, and there could be a biological deficiency militating against benevolence (Harari, 2014) – it is difficult to avoid

DOI: 10.1057/9781137468468.0006

contact with others within the close proximity of family, work place and dole queue, the Joycean street, civil and uncivil society. The argument for moral economy is that it conduces to intersubjective social relations, promoting the bonds of Durkheimian social solidarity and universality. So, theoretically and empirically, it conduces to self-preservation and is in the enlightened best interests of all of us (Wilkinson and Pickett, 2009). The weight of evidence suggests that more equal societies almost always do better on a range of social indicators – mental illness and drug use, ill-health and lower life expectancy, obesity, educational perform-ance, including *violence, crime, punishment and imprisonment*. When confronted with the strength of this evidence the logical implication is to reduce elongated hierarchies, the acme of which is occupied by the elite comptrollers of the material universe. Inequality creates dysfunc-tional societies through the production of social pathologies rooted in material differences. Of the major economies in Europe none are more unequal than Britain (Piketty, 2014). For Hippodamos, in classical antiquity, the individual achieves happiness and perfection in a group 'for the individual and the community are coterminous' (Blumenfeld, 2001: 181). This moral code informed Pauline political ethics with its existential burden to reconstruct the polis. In fact, the political ethics of Romans 12v9 –13v7 is a manual of moral excellence that 'connects the individual's proper end with the collective end' (Blumenfeld, 2001: 386). This is the Hegelian point that morality appertains to social organisa-tion, not the will to power of atomistic individuals at the expense of others (Plant, 1973).

The argument advanced is that the content of moral economy establishes normative principles, intellectually supported ground rules, that are not only good in themselves but facilitate the good life for all citizens (Aristotle, 2000). There is an ethico-cultural tradition connect-ing Hippodamos, Aristotle, Pauline ethics, Schweitzer, Wilkinson and Pickett. This tradition includes Küng whose global ethic establishes minimum 'human values, criteria and basic attitudes' (1998: 92). It is a matter of wisdom, logic, rationality and aesthetics to endorse moral economy, in contradistinction to capitalist political economy, as a normative code of virtue by which to get ourselves organised. Klein (2014), from a psychological perspective, argues that living within the circuits of moral economy make us feel better about ourselves. This reso-nates with Plato's *Republic* (1974) where justice (δικαιοσύνη) is beneficial to psychic health. In other words, the just or moral person is happier

DOI: 10.1057/9781137468468.0006

than the unjust. Additionally, Pinker (2015), a developmental psychologist, has undertaken empirical research that supports the position that the Internet age makes us unhappy. It is damaging our social natures, isolating us from each other through pseudo-superficial human contacts and relations. Philosophically, theologically, sociologically and psychologically, it is better to give than receive, good begets good, and virtue is its own reward. The supporting arguments for moral economy direct our thinking towards political ethics where they were located in classical antiquity. Regardless of moral debates, the diversity of ethical systems and aetiological questions, it seems a good idea, a matter of practical reason, to consider moral economy as a foundational life-view. To do otherwise is stupid because it detracts from the possibility of human happiness and the good life for all. Put simply, we need each other.

By reflecting on these supportive arguments, the opportunity is presented to move from the *world as it is* to *what it could be*. The intellectual resources on morality synthesised in the previous chapter, and the content of and arguments for moral economy under consideration here, offer us half a chance to live together through sharing in the abundance of the world's material, intellectual and ethico-cultural resources. Cooperation not barbaric competition make us more rather than less human, leading to growth of refined sensibilities and an enhanced understanding of each other, including criminal behavioural repertoires (Hall, 2012). Of course, the formulation of content and articulation of argument will not convince everyone, easily dismissed as an irrelevant distraction from life's material priorities and obsession with economic growth. The objection is that the content is unrealistic and supportive arguments unconvincing, passé and unmodern. The Nietzschean Übermensch is contemptuous of virtuous egalitarian neighbourliness and equality. It represents an ethic that degrades the human stock that must be transcended into a higher form of aristocratic life through the will to power. The Nietzschean emphasis is aesthetics not ethics and, as Kenny elucidates, Nietzsche's 'ideal human being not only does not love his neighbour: he has no neighbour' (2010: 939).

We can turn to intellectual considerations of moral economy not only to critique the present but also inform existential decisions about the future. Political, social and economic organisation should not be reduced to technical specificities, computer modelling, cost–benefit analyses or risk assessment. From Plato and Aristotle, Paul and Hegel, to Keynes and Piketty, these are intellectual and moral matters that are

DOI: 10.1057/9781137468468.0006

foundationally required to promote the general welfare over self-interest which has implications for the rationality of criminal justice. The weight of evidence suggests that this has never happened and it is the last thing we want, even after the material crisis of 2007–08. Mumford (1940: 572), berating the limitations of liberalism, stated that 'universal principles and values give purpose and direction to human life'. Furthermore, Sandel argues that a 'politics of moral engagement is not only a more inspiring ideal than a politics of avoidance. It is also a more promising basis for a just society' (2009: 269). From these general comments let us turn to the specifics of criminal justice.

As with content, so too with argument, the contours of morality operated in the circuits of the criminal justice system, an important (by no means only) source was the probation ideal and rehabilitative ethic. This was a central reproductive and state supported mechanism which is disrupted by applying market-driven concepts to organisational structures that previously transcended market operations. There was a moral dynamic to probation practice exemplified in the dialectics of criminal justice that pursued truth and justice through dialogic argument. There is no political philosophy of left or right, criminological theory, or organisational component of the system – magistrates, judges, clerks, solicitors, barristers, crown prosecution service, police or probation – that can rightfully claim a monopoly on truth and justice. Nevertheless, each organisation with its unique historical formation, professional culture, primary task and reproductive ethico-cultural mechanisms can combine dialectically to advance different perspectives on the meaning of criminal and social justice. Organisational contestation conduces to negotiated outcomes through contradiction, argument and sometimes conflict (more so than collapsing differences through reducing *cultural divides* which terminates in the bland leading the bland; see Chapter 3 on the National Offender Management Service). Any justice system that overly relied on prosecution evidence supplied to magistrates' and crown court judges from the police and crown prosecution service, would provoke a serious challenge to truth, justice and fairness because of what it omitted by being reductively concerned only with *what* the offender has done. Equally, to rely solely on a personalist ideology, social work explanations, respect for persons in some ideal kingdom of ends, would be rightly challenged by victims and local communities according to the same demand for truth, justice and fairness. Consequently, the argument is that both perspectives are required, *what* someone has

DOI: 10.1057/9781137468468.0006

done as well as understanding *why*. But this delicate balance has been unbalanced by modernisation *from above*, excessive political interference, a permanent revolution of repeated organisational restructuring, the erosion of sociological analyses and the hollowing out of intellectual and ethico-cultural exploration. This transformation is contingent upon the decline of the probation ideal, the rehabilitative ethic and supporting intellectual and moral arguments. The system has shifted from the dialectics of negotiated outcomes operating within a contested space, to a reductionist politics of coercive imposition by the political class for strategic reasons rather than the primary cause of justice. Thinking about doing justice is structured within political and fiscal parameters, but it must also be informed by the intellectual and moral resources assembled in Chapter 1. If not, then the foundations of criminal and social justice will be undermined, as assuredly they have been. To do what is just and right self-evidently requires intellectual curiosity and moral sensibility. Probation was a guarantor of this vital perspective, but no longer because it has been declared out of time, out of step and out of sorts with the latest *great transformation* of the state. Amartya Sen (2009), invoking Adam Smith (1759/2009), with a trace of Joyce and Eliot, argues that reasoned and critical scrutiny, to accommodate different intellectual positions, is a basic requirement for ethical and political conviction. The need to 'transcend the limitations of our positional perspectives is important in moral and political philosophy, and in jurisprudence' (Sen 2009, 155). Public reasoning, critical discussion, listening to and learning from others and assimilating different viewpoints, is central to the intellectual and moral process of criminal and social justice.

Mode of conceptualisation and articulation

Like Eagleton's (2014) disquisition on God or Lacan and Žižek on the Symbolic (Big Other), moral economy is ambiguous, sometimes unrecognisable, betrays a mythical quality and it does not readily elicit assent to its entreaties. However, it has the capacity to challenge, disturb and disrupt behavioural routines and organisational rationalities. It is not part of nature, or in its nature, to impose itself coercively in the manner of Nietzschean will to power. Rather, it is subtle in its intimation and invitation through its scattered historical and contemporary deposits. It takes issue with the way the world is, the images we construct of the

DOI: 10.1057/9781137468468.0006

self that reflect and reproduce the neoliberal politico-economic order with its material signs, status symbols and all too ephemeral definitions of success. It allows itself to be pushed out of the world, onto a cross, towards the extremity of the inexplicable Real beyond the Symbolic. It does not, never has, probably never will, effect a permanent revolution in human affairs as it is easily deflected and often defeated although never permanently expunged, again like Eagleton's God. The crushing weight of history and present arrangements are stacked against it. Moral economy, like the Pauline politico-ethical state (Blumenfeld, 2001: 389) did not constitute a threat to the Roman Empire, because it operated as a parallel not usurpatory state, but with the efficacy to be transformative. It disturbs, disarms and comforts the human condition, yet it is a paradox because the content of moral economy is not averse to making an egregious appearance on celebratory state occasions. At the National Service of Thanksgiving to mark the Diamond Jubilee of Her Majesty the Queen, in Saint Paul's Cathedral on Tuesday 5 June 2012, the blessing from the Archbishop of Canterbury enjoined the departing congregation to function within the circuits of moral economy: go forth into the world in peace; be of good courage; hold fast that which is good; render to no one evil for evil; strengthen the fainthearted and support the weak; help the afflicted and honour everyone. Expeditiously, state power vacated the sacred pew to sustain the material platform, as the reproduction of exchange relations continues its relentless march in maintaining inequality and injustice throughout the social structure.

Moral economy is imperceptible and ineffable, but affective, expressive and sometimes practiced, as not all relations between human beings are exchange relations. Hume acknowledged that human beings are not solely motivated by self-interest. There are a thousand instances which are the 'marks of a general benevolence in human nature' (1777/1983: 92). Similarly, Smith (1759/2009: 48) endorsed the pleasing social passions of generosity, kindness and compassion. It should be repeated that moral economy, like political economy, does not intrinsically belong to the structure of the world. It relies on the renewal of existential commitment to its distinctive content and supportive arguments. It can be avoided, we can look the other way, heave our shoulder against it. We can choose an alternative course of action and fill the void at the core of human existence with an alternative symbolic content. There are many competitors clamouring for our attention in the market place of ideological lifestyles. But in doing so we must face the consequences of our actions that

DOI: 10.1057/9781137468468.0006

will inevitably follow. The threads of moral economy, like the veneer of civilisation, have a tenuous hold over the human condition and can all too quickly slide into barbarism. It is insecure and impermanent unless defended, advocated and advanced by all of us in our personal relations, the organisation of the polis and organisational forms of life that include the criminal justice system.

Schweitzer's life-view of reverence for life transcended the savage conflict enjoined by the Triple Entente against the Triple Alliance of Central Powers in the First World War, but it was not the platform for the post-war reconstruction in Europe, nor did it prevent World War Two. However, the intellectual community would profit from re-acquaintance with *Civilisation and Ethics* (1929). Bonhoeffer's work on *Ethics* (1955) did not save the German state or Church in the 1930s, nor did it defeat racism or even prevent his own execution in April 1945, yet his theological and Christological legacy survives to inform thinking about morality in this monograph. The Judaeo-Christian ethic did not transform the Roman Empire of the Caesars. It did not create a new world order based upon a political ethic of agapē, or usher in the Kingdom of God because it ended in 'defeat' on a cross. But there are those who conduct their lives according to its code and bear witness to its efficacy to transform existence through immersion in a new Symbolic order. This intellectual, ethico-cultural legacy informs the outputs of Badiou and Žižek. It may not be feasible to imagine a perfect state of moral economy rather than capitalist political economy. It is, however, more feasible to factor the deposits of moral economy into discussions on political organisation to analyse, critique and to offer alternative perspectives. This will not be a comfortable ride. Furthermore, the content of, arguments for and the mode of conceptualisation and articulation of moral economy has implications for the criminal justice system. Accordingly, the intellectual resources on morality assembled in Chapter 1, and specific attention directed towards the conceptual device of moral economy in Chapter 2, must now be put to work.

Note

1   The American Friends Service Committee (1971) said it was theoretically faulty, systematically discriminatory and inconsistent with the principles of justice. It put needs before deeds, it could be arbitrary and oppressive,

DOI: 10.1057/9781137468468.0006

relied too much on 'experts' who imposed 'solutions', welfare tyrannical because it forced people to be cured, denied respect and responsibility to individuals, detained people in prison for longer than was necessary through indeterminate sentences. Furthermore, it 'didn't work' as research in the 1970s revealed: Lipton, Martinson and Wilks (1975); Martinson (1974); IMPACT (Folkard, 1974 and 1976); Brody (1976). However, it symbolically represented welfare and personalist ideals. See Allen (1981); Cullen and Gilbert (1982).

DOI: 10.1057/9781137468468.0006

3
Moral Economy, Criminal Justice and Probation: From 1979 to 2010

Abstract: *This chapter puts moral economy to work in the criminal justice system, with specific consideration awarded to probation. I am directly concerned to explore the changing coordinates of the system of justice from 1979–92, 1992–97 and 1997–2010. This 31 year period incorporates conservative (18 years) and New Labour (13 years) administrations. The central task is to expose criminal justice to the charge of moral vacuity, contingent upon repeated political assaults on probation, particularly after 1992.*

Whitehead, Philip. *Reconceptualising the Moral Economy of Criminal Justice: A New Perspective.* Basingstoke: Palgrave Macmillan, 2015. DOI: 10.1057/9781137468468.0007.

This chapter does not provide a detailed account of probation, criminal justice and penal policy between 1979 and 2010. Much of the necessary spadework has already been undertaken (Burke and Collett, 2014; Canton, 2011; Faulkner and Burnett, 2012; Faulkner, 2014; Garland, 1985 and 2001; Mair and Burke, 2012; Mawby and Worrall, 2013; Whitehead and Statham, 2006; Whitehead, 2010). Rather, my main task is to reframe the intellectual and moral transformation of criminal justice through the revelatory index of probation. Writing immediately prior to the parameter of interest in this chapter to establish a point of contrast, Haxby observed correctly that the 'probation and after-care service has never been free from change, but at present it is at a crucial stage in its development. Many changes have been imposed on it recently by legislation and administrative decision, and other changes are pending' (1978: 15). Furthermore, by splicing the *Review of Criminal Justice Policy* (Home Office, 1977) to Haxby's analysis, the following features are worthy of historical notation:

▸ Beginning in 1966, probation assumed responsibility for welfare posts in prisons, and the Advisory Council on the Penal System (ACPS) was established.

▸ The Criminal Justice Act 1967 renamed probation the Probation and After-Care Service to reflect its expanding duties in the criminal justice system.

▸ In 1968, parole was introduced which signified the ideological continuity with a prison system orientated towards rehabilitation, both during and beyond custodial release. Also, at this juncture, the Seebohm Committee presented probation with an acute dilemma: if probation rejected proposals to become part of the reorganised local authority social services departments, it risked isolation from mainstream social work and closer identification with the penal system. By contrast, if it cooperated it risked assimilation, the loss of identity and autonomy as a separate service (precisely the dilemma facing the third sector between 2010 and 2015 as we shall see later).

▸ The Children and Young Persons Act 1969 marked the apotheosis of the welfare and treatment model for young offenders that complemented the rehabilitative ideal that anchored adult criminal justice services. Probation assumed responsibility for social work posts in remand centres, detention centres and borstal allocation centres, but not borstals themselves as housemasters retained relevant responsibilities before becoming managers in due course.

DOI: 10.1057/9781137468468.0007

▶ By 1970 plans were afoot to expand further probation responsibilities and, in 1971, Central Council for the Education and Training in Social Work (CCETSW) was established under whose auspices I trained as a probation officer (as a *social worker of the courts*) at Lancaster University during 1979–81, alongside local authority social work and psychiatric social work students.

▶ The Criminal Justice Act 1972 introduced the Community Service Order. Additionally, and importantly, probation asserted its determination to retain its identity as a separate organisation following Seebohm. The central government grant increased from 50% to 80% and the separation of probation from local government was completed in the 1980s when it became fully funded.

▶ The Powers of the Criminal Courts Act 1973 and the pilot of community service schemes commenced in six areas.

▶ 1974 IMPACT (Folkard et al., 1974 and 1976) questioned the rehabilitative efficacy of probation practice, and Brody (1976) the deterrent effects of sentencing. Furthermore, the Younger Report on Young Adult Offenders accentuated debates over care and control and the future direction of probation. Local government reorganisation resulted in probation areas being reduced from 79 to 56.

▶ By 1975 there was a worsening economic climate which restricted the expansion of probation, even though Probation Committees were given the opportunity to introduce community service schemes in their local areas.

The *Review* (Home Office, 1977) constitutes a site of historical interest for students of criminal justice, but of greater interest is the tonal quality of its policy formulations. Not only, in conjunction with Haxby, does it summarise salient developmental turning points before 1979 in penal policy affecting probation, prisons and the police, it also provides insights into the philosophico-cultural platform of government towards criminal justice. Although the 1970s were increasingly afflicted by fiscal pressure in a more competitive global economy, policies towards criminal justice reflected economic contingencies *and* humanitarian concerns (Home Office, 1977: 3). The humanitarian dimension was manifested in Home Office support for probation work in conjunction with attempts to reduce the prison population. For example, in 1975 the average daily prison population in prisons, detention centres and borstal combined was approximately 40,000 (Berman and Dar, 2013); by 1980 it was 43,109. The commitment to reduce the prison population remained a feature of

DOI: 10.1057/9781137468468.0007

government policy until the early 1990s. It was acknowledged that custo-dial sentences have a deterrent effect, but they can also inflict damage on young offenders and must be avoided where possible. Government policy towards, and organisational practices within, the criminal justice system were approaching the historical juncture when economy and effi-ciency, value for money, managerial and bureaucratic rationality, would assume greater significance than formerly. However, rehabilitation remained the hegemonic ideology (although increasingly questioned by research), probation had a significant role in criminal and social justice and the system aspired to reduce the prison population. *They did things differently then, and thought and felt differently.* Furthermore, the *Review* acknowledged that the causes of crime cannot be detached from prevail-ing structural political, social and economic conditions. However, this detachment increasingly occurred from the 1980s as the tightening grip of neoliberalism and neoconservatism displaced Keynesian polity. Additionally, the doctrine of individual responsibility found its crimi-nological expression in the tenets of neoclassical and administrative criminology.

The general election in May 1979 may well have signalled a politico-economic fracture with the post-war consensus, but caution is required when analysing criminal justice. Indubitably, Thatcherism proceeded to reconfigure relations between central and local government, the state and citizen, public and private sectors, but Farrall and Jennings (2014) advance a nuanced analysis of criminality and criminal justice. The evidence to excavate the 1980s is replete with paradox as it reveals conti-nuity *and* discontinuity with the previous decade, differences of degree rather than kind. Although an insider's account reveals that during the 1980s criminal justice policies, procedures and practices became more politicised, it was also described by some as an 'Indian summer of liberal criminal justice policy' (Faulkner, 2014: 89; see also Stewart, 2013). The conservative government was elected on a platform of fiscal probity and market discipline that affected the domains of social security, education, housing policy and attitudes towards the family. Moreover, criminal justice became entangled in the erosion of the post-war Keynesian consensus, the web of economic decline, rising crime, the disenchant-ment with treatment and rehabilitation, and *the great moving right show* (Hall and Jacques, 1983). Windlesham (1993: 144) boldly refers to the ascendency of conservative populist and pugilist law and order politics following the decline of liberal–democratic culture,[1] but overstates his

DOI: 10.1057/9781137468468.0007

case. Of course, we know from autobiographical disclosures that the conservatives were led by a prime minister with uncompromising views on crime. In her autobiographical *The Path to Power* (1995) she revealed her indebtedness to the criminological mentorship of E. Van Den Haag and J.Q. Wilson who advocated neoclassicism, individual responsibility, retributive and deterrent punishments, which assaulted sociological theory to facilitate aetiological explorations. Farrall and Jennings (2014: 211) argue that she wanted people to feel safe walking the streets, was intellectually committed to law and order, blamed social workers for mitigating criminality and favoured capital punishment. Accordingly these 'sentiments can be interpreted as a desire for a criminal justice system which did not embrace penal welfare, favoured crime control models of policing and which tended towards harsher penalties' (2014: 212). But the evidence is analytically complex and demands the separation of personal predisposition from the policies and practices her governments and Home Secretaries pursued.

Penologically on the right of her first Home Secretary William Whitelaw who eschewed extremist politics (Windlesham, 1993: 159), Mrs. Thatcher uncompromisingly asserted that 'the most direct way to act against crime is to make life as difficult as possible for the potential and actual criminal' (1995: 558). However, the bark of criminological affiliation exceeded bite, rhetoric trumped the reality of what in fact occurred, evidenced by the mediating liberal influences of Whitelaw; the legislative restrictions on custodial sentences for young people contained in the Criminal Justice Act 1982 and, subsequently, the Criminal Justice Act 1991 by which time she had left office. Moreover, the Police and Criminal Evidence Act 1984 gave rights to suspects and the prison population fell for a short period after 1988. Indeed, as prime minister she 'presided over a government that was seriously committed to reducing the use of imprisonment ...' (Faulkner, 2014: 139). Therefore, it is evidentially suggestive that criminal justice during this period was characterised more by consensus and continuity than the politics of radical Thatcherism. During the 1980s there was no radical lurch to the penological right.

Nevertheless, there was a *turn of significance* after 1982 that was more fiscal than penological, as the Financial Management Initiative (FMI) promoted governmental objectives conducive to creating a performance culture, and yielding more accurate information on costs. These principles were introduced into probation during 1983–84 through the

DOI: 10.1057/9781137468468.0007

Statement of National Objectives and Priorities (SNOP) that signalled the opportunity to establish more consistent, accountable and efficient practices throughout area services. This situated probation policies and practices within a clearer fiscal framework where economic priorities supposedly determined policy, not policy (no matter how axiologically and morally praiseworthy and value orientated) determining resources. Although money can be found and spent for political advantage – CCTV, electronic tagging, 'war on drugs' – the message emanating from the Home Office was that organisations must operate within defined budget parameters. The responses to SNOP from the 56 local proba-tion areas (Lloyd, 1986) were instructive in revealing perceptions of, and commitments to, probation history and culture that had congealed over preceding decades. The disparate responses also demonstrated dissonance between probation area practices and political priorities that, inadvertently, provided the Home Office with the empirical evidence to justify the message of consistency articulated in the Statement. It was acknowledged by one probation area that probation values should not be subjected to financial accounting methodologies, which exposed a fault line between organisational culture and political priorities, and instru-mental and substantive rationality with its smattering of deontological ethics. The notable changes were fiscal rather than penological and by 1986 the Home Office commissioned Deloitte, Haskins and Sells to develop a Financial Management Information System to ensure progress towards the 3Es of economy, efficiency and effectiveness, including value for money (VfM) which was already being applied in other public serv-ices such as the civil service, health, local authorities, police, prisons and schools (Humphrey, 1987: 23; Whittington, 1988: 205).

On the 28 September 1987, a Home Office seminar was held at Leeds Castle in Kent, presided over by Douglas Hurd (Home Secretary from September 1985 to October 1989). The event covered the whole range of Home Office business, and was attended by all ministers, Brian Cubbon, the Permanent Secretary, and senior officials including Mary Tuck, Head of Research and Planning, and David Faulkner, Deputy Under-Secretary of state. The themes under discussion were crime prevention and safer cities, sentencing policy and probation, and preventing young people becoming enmeshed in the adult criminal justice system. There was growing alarm at the prison population – 43,109 in 1980; 50,000 in September 1987; and the projected figure was 60,000–70,000 by 2000 which was deemed politically, fiscally and presumably morally

DOI: 10.1057/9781137468468.0007

unacceptable (but not by 1992–93). The seminar was instrumental in forging a strategy for criminal justice that enhanced the appeal of community sentences to magistrates and judges, and probation would have a central role in the delivery of punishment in the community. It should also be recalled that Douglas Hurd was not unsympathetic to the work and values of probation. Towards the end of the 1980s (see Shaw and Haines, 1989), although probation work had been built upon social work foundations and its officers had been social workers of the criminal and civil courts, this was no longer considered a credible ideological platform upon which to justify its continued existence. The deliberations at Leeds Castle contributed to *Punishment, Custody and Community 1988* (Green Paper), the forerunner to the Criminal Justice Act 1991.[2]

When excavating the twists and turns, continuities and discontinuities, in criminal justice during the 1980s, compared to the preceding period, it is pertinent to frame the discussion by constructing analytical categories of intellectual and moral relevance under the headings of legislation, administrative–bureaucratic, state control and the politico-economic as follows:

1 Legislative developments – CJA 1982, Police and Criminal Evidence Act 1984, Public Order Act 1986, CJA 1987, 1988 and 1991. This is legislatively modest compared to what happened after 1997 (see Ministry of Justice, 2013g).
2 Administrative, managerial and bureaucratic expansion to refine and enhance the mechanisms of central fiscal control over organisations in the form of cash limits, FMI, SNOP, 3Es and VfM (see Audit Commission Report, 1989; National Audit Office, 1989).
3 Restructuring the nexus of state, public sector, private interests, fiscal demands and political control through the New Public Management (NPM).
4 The platform of political, social and economic transformations, from the post-war Keynesian social democratic consensus from the 1950s to 1970s, to neoliberal and neoconservative principles since the 1980s.

Amplifying the last point, by the late 1980s the New Public Management (Faulkner and Burnett, 2012: 168; Hood, 1991) was characterised by the reduction in professional autonomy and discretion; separate purchasing of services from their provision; measurable outcomes not service outputs; a performance culture of fiscal rewards for success and penalties

DOI: 10.1057/9781137468468.0007

for failure (precursor to Payment by Results); contracts and managerial consultants, commercial transactions in a more business-orientated environment; private sector rationality extended to the public sector; downgrade the role of civil servants, professionals and academics in the criminal justice policy process. Furthermore, when turning to the *state, public, private, fiscal nexus* Windlesham refers to the situation in 1987 to privatise court escort services, and the greater involvement of the private sector in prisons (1993: 278–79; see chapter 9 Faulkner's *Servant of the Crown*). Hurd moved in the direction of privatisation when casting the net towards the skills and knowledge that existed within the private sector, particularly to supervise the prison building programme and to accelerate delivery. The conservative members of the House of Commons Affairs Committee had recommended, as an experiment, private sector companies bidding for the construction and management of custodial institutions, influenced by what was happening in the United States on private prisons (Jones and Newburn, 2007; see also Whitehead and Crawshaw, 2012). This reflects the ideological commitment towards privatisation and corresponding reduction in the role of the public sector that became much more penetrative during 2010 to 2015.

From 1992 to 1997

If the period from 1979 to the early 1990s requires nuanced analysis, 1992 to 1997 precipitated intellectual questions and moral disquiet appertaining to the political restructuring of criminal justice and penal policy. Although Windlesham (1993: 207) commented on the speedy turn of events in the 1980s, the pace discernibly quickened in the 1990s. John Major became prime minister on the 28 November.1990, further progress was made in the direction of cash limits in 1991, and on the 9 April 1992 the conservatives won a fourth consecutive general election. Philippa Drew, Head of the Home Office Probation Division, confidently stated, 'I personally think that the service has a great future in both its criminal and civil work' (in Whitehead and Statham, 2006: 131). Events conspired to take a different turn. After 1992–93 previous attempts from within the Home Office by Douglas Hurd, John Patten and David Faulkner to forge a rational criminal justice policy expressed in the Criminal Justice Act 1991, was subjected to a volte face of dramatic import. This was a troubled period that lamented the murder of Jamie Bulger in February 1993,

DOI: 10.1057/9781137468468.0007

followed by Stephen Lawrence in April. Substantively, the Criminal Justice Act 1993 undermined key intentions of the 1991 Act (see Note 2 at end of Chapter 3 on CJA 1991 and 1993). Recorded crime had risen to 5.38m in 1992, from 2.38m in 1979, and the economic situation was giving cause for concern. The isobars narrowed to create a political storm that battered probation and criminal justice, and it is conspiratorially suggested that the conservative government manipulated the law and order agenda in response to the Exchange Rate Mechanism fiasco of 16 September 1992 (Farrall and Jennings, 2014; also Whitehead and Statham, 2006: 132).[3]

In October 1993 Home Secretary Howard announced his 27-point plan on law and order, using the party conference platform to signal a radical break in criminal justice and penal policy. Approximately four weeks later David Faulkner (1993) composed a letter to the Guardian newspaper, the burden of which expressed disquiet at the emerging reactionary attitude within the Home Office towards criminalisation, punishment and prison that reconfigured intellectual and moral conventions. For decades the traditional sources of received wisdom were the deliberations of advisory bodies, commissions, the collective wisdom of civil servants, professionals within their respective organisations and consultation with university academics (see Marquand, 2014 on the decline of the professional service elite and code of honour, civic duty, values and stable decision-making structures). It was a shift in democratic convention from government by discussion, consultation and public reason that represented a broad constituency of interests (Sen, 2009), to a narrower platform controlled by a central political core. It opened up an intellectual and moral void.

This is a critical juncture in the ethico-cultural reframing of criminal justice policy and practice *from above* that was exacerbated under New Labour after 1997. The heightened political emphasis on criminalisation, detection, conviction, punishment and prison manifested a more viscerally expressive Durkheimian tone, alongside more penetrative managerial and Weberian bureaucratic procedures. Populist expressivism and bureaucratic intrusion forged an unlikely alliance that outflanked the intellectual and moral conventions of criminal justice and penal policy. When Faulkner expressed disquiet at the void being created he was alluding to the abandonment of a more settled, democratic and rational process that had operated within the Home Office. The situation was further exacerbated in the 1995 Green Paper *Strengthening Punishment in the Community* that proposed a new sentence of the court. Windlesham (2001: 4–5) observed that expressive penal rhetoric was in

DOI: 10.1057/9781137468468.0007

the ascendancy over intellectual and moral substance which exposed Howard to the charge of 'cynical opportunism' that drowned out the voices of reason and moral sensibility. It can be argued that the politics of coercive imposition, centrally imposed mechanisms of command and control, strategic governmental tactics over the evidence on penological effectiveness, delivered through the ex-cathedra statements from governments with a 'we know best' attitude, inflicted serious damage on the settled procedures for formulating criminal justice and penal policy. It is not possible to imagine the state's investment in the operations of criminal justice functioning without taking cognisance of the prevailing politico-economic platform, material priorities and ideological convictions, legislative parameters, administrative mechanisms and the aforementioned nexus of interests. But, equally, the state has a democratic responsibility to operate within clearly defined intellectual and moral indicators just as much as key performance indicators. Without the former, criminal justice is exposed then relegated into the Real of political and economic contingency. Farrall and Jennings (2014: 227–28) pull together a number of strands in their analysis: neoliberalism and neoconservatism to advance an explanatory account of crime and criminal justice; the context of changing structural determinants, public and media attitudes and government responses to events. Accordingly, the '1990s was one such period, as long-term trends in crime rates, combined with increasing public concern about the importance of the issue of crime (as well as increased interparty competition over their law and order credentials), contributed to demand for policy solutions and tougher measures on criminal justice' (2014: 227–28).

A final word on the 1995 document *Strengthening Punishment in the Community* that proposed a new sentence because of ongoing concerns that probation was increasingly perceived as a soft sentencing option despite considerable repositioning over recent years. The Home Office wanted to give the courts a controlling interest over the content of community sentences. Additionally, Howard's conference speech at Blackpool in 1995 advocated putting honesty back into sentencing to ensure the prison term served was closer to the sentence passed; focus on victims more than offenders; longer sentences for violent, sexual offenders and burglars; and minimum sentences that culminated in the *Crime (Sentences) Act 1997* popularly known as the 'two and three strikes legislation'. This legislation reversed earlier efforts to reduce imprisonment. However, these developments must be qualified by the *Two*

DOI: 10.1057/9781137468468.0007

Demonstration Projects that were trialed during 1995 in Cleveland and Shropshire with the intention of giving existing legislation a chance to be effective (Home Office, 1999). Concurrently, the decision was taken on the future of probation training that detached probation history, work and cultural tradition from social work and the personal social services. Home Office sponsorship of the *Diploma in Social Work* ceased in 1995–96 and probation did not produce any new recruits for the next four years. The Diploma in Probation Studies was introduced in 1998 (Whitehead and Thompson, 2004). Shortly before the general election of the 1 May 1997, I recall being on court duty at the Teesside Magistrates' Court. During the course of the afternoon's proceedings the news surfaced that Labour's election battle bus, with Mr. Blair on board, was parked alongside the central library in close proximity to the court. Curiosity got the better of the legal profession as probation officers, solicitors and court clerks stepped outside to ponder whether we were witnessing the beginnings of a new dispensation for criminal justice after the punitive disruptions since the early 1990s. Perhaps a return to the 'gentler' tone of the aforementioned Labour government's 1976 *Review* document was imminent. How wrong and naïve we were; there would be no social work transformation of the politics of punishment.

From 1997 to 2010

New Labour was elected to office on the 1 May 1997 with a majority of 179 parliamentary seats and, continuous with previous conservative administrations, operated a paradoxical criminal justice and penal policy that was a mélange of inconsistency. There was no ceremonial abandonment of the empirical linkage between adverse socioeconomic conditions and criminal behaviour included in the *Review* under 'old' labour (Home Office, 1977). But nor did New Labour dilute the salience attached to punishment and prison that featured prominently after 1992–93. Helena Kennedy commented: 'That Labour took the decision to continue Michael Howard's incarceration binge is one of the blackest marks against the government's record on social justice' (2005: 283). Tonry (2004) accused Labour of knowingly adopting policies that were demonstrably ineffective that exposed the fault line running through the demand for penological effectiveness and the politics of usefulness in the dark arts of strategic government. There would be no attenuation of New

DOI: 10.1057/9781137468468.0007

Public Management and the privatisation agenda. The problematic of probation within the new punitive dispensation remained a conundrum alongside support for restorative justice which did not signal a return to welfare, social work and the personal social services. There could be no going back to the tone of the *Review* of the late 1970s, rather more of the same since 1993. Equally, there was no return to the Keynesian consensus, but a deregulated neoliberal political economy which had functional implications for the criminal justice system (Wacquant, 2009). The *unique selling point* of New Labour was the mission to modernise: 'We must be tough; we must be modern; we must get value for money; we must be re-elected' (Cavadino and Dignan, 2006: 75). Transformations in criminal justice, indexed specifically in probation, elicited the view that it had become unrecognisable and unimaginable to its early beginnings in the late 19th and early 20th centuries (Chui and Nellis, 2003: 10). In fact, New Labour policies from 1997 continued the focus on the ethico-cultural deficiencies of individuals and families, not structural-material conditions under capitalism. Policy focused on the fast tracking of young offenders, Anti-Social Behaviour Orders and the 'war against crime' that divides citizens in the polis as a strategy for promoting social solidarity against the relegated other. All these matters can be reframed as precipitating intellectual and moral concern.

New Labour would have accrued considerable credit for initiating a review of the intellectual and moral landscape of criminal justice policy and practice after 18 years of conservative administrations. Instead, one of the first acts of the Home Office under Jack Straw in July 1997 was to announce the *Prisons–Probation Review*. This signalled an aspiration to conflate these two organisations to improve performance and effectiveness, but at the risk of blurring the distinctions of separate histories, traditions, primary tasks, training, requisite skills, as well as the uncodified process of cultural transmission and inculcation of values from one generation of staff to the next. The political goal was to *reduce cultural divides* between probation and prison, when an equally cogent argument can be advanced to maintain separate yet complimentary identities and functions to advance the dialectics of criminal and social justice. In 1998, the year that the new probation training system began (Whitehead and Thompson, 2004), the Home Office published *Joining Forces To Protect The Public: Prisons–Probation* consultation document which revealed that the suggested merger would not occur (not yet). Nevertheless, New Labour worked towards the creation of a modernised probation service

DOI: 10.1057/9781137468468.0007

that began on the 1 April 2001. According to Windlesham (2001: 238), New Labour's modernisation programme contained three substantive elements:

▸ More emphasis on the enforcement of court orders that transformed probation into a law-enforcement agency, an adjunct of punishment in the community
▸ Creating the National Probation Service
▸ Creating a new Family Court Welfare Service (Children and Family Court Advisory and Support Service (CAFCASS))

Additionally, a review of the courts began in 1999 under Lord Justice Auld. Then, during 1999–2000, Youth Offending Teams were established that culminated in probation becoming an agency for adult offenders. Modernisation accelerated legislative expansion as there were 66 new pieces of legislation between 1995 and 2007 (Solomon et al., 2007). There was no reversal of the neoliberal politico-economic platform, and the further expansion of administrative–managerial–bureaucratic mechanisms of central command and control were clearly illustrated in the construction of the National Probation Service. The Halliday review of sentencing began on 16 May 2000 and culminated in the Criminal Justice Act 2003. Importantly, the Carter review of correctional services that commenced in March 2002 established the National Offender Management Service (NOMS) in 2003–04. Two specific illustrations of intellectual and moral concern should be noted from within this transformative culture that included the emergence of the Ministry of Justice in 2007, and transition from caring to punitive control in proba-tion (Burnett et al., 2007: 228. See also Faulkner and Burnett, 2012 on successes and failures of New Labour).[4]

First, the Carter report (2003) that established NOMS achieved what was not possible in 1997–98. This is because it was first necessary to create the National Probation Service to enhance central command and control. The rationale for bringing prisons and probation together was to improve end-to-end management, enhance performance and effective-ness, continue the penetration of the 3Es, and to establish a platform of contestability to open up criminal justice services to a mixed economy of public, private and voluntary enterprises (see Chapter 4). Creating a mixed economy of provision was not innovative as Fullwood (1994) alluded to challenges to the monopoly position of probation from a pluralism of providers. Additionally, reference has already been made to the early stages of privatisation in the 1980s, but NOMS constituted a decisive move in this direction, legislatively consolidated in the *Offender Management Act 2007*. Further reforms to NOMS were initiated during 2008–09 (Carter, 2007) to coordinate and commission all probation and prison services from the public, private and voluntary sectors. This was the operational platform established by 2010 and the election of a coalition government.

The second intellectual and moral concern, eventually abandoned, was the withdrawal of state benefit from offenders between the age of 18 and 59 subject to a community order and prosecuted for non-compliance, under ss62–66 of the Child Support, Pensions and Social Security Act 2000. The policy was piloted in four areas of which Teesside was one. The rationale was to ensure compliance to a community order by the punitive threat of withdrawal of all or part of benefit for up to four weeks. Helena Kennedy evaluated that the cost of processing each benefit sanction case through the Magistrates' Court was £730, but the amount saved by activating the sanction was £132 per case. She proceeded to state that 'Inventing new ways to punish the poor is a disgraceful activity for a Labour government' (2005: 245).

First summation: intellectual and moral disturbances

This chapter begins the task of reframing intellectual and moral transformations in criminal justice from 1979 to 2010 (31 years). It draws attention to legislative developments and centrally imposed administrative, managerial and bureaucratic mechanisms of control. It also alludes to the platform of neoliberal capitalism that displaced the Keynesian welfare–social state, and organisational restructuring through New Public Management that recalibrated the balance between the public and private interest. During the 1980s there was limited criminal justice activity in the direction of the *great moving right show*, notwithstanding the criminological credentials of the conservative prime minister. Tonal comparisons can be made with the 1960s and 1970s (Home Office, 1977), but they are fiscal and administrative rather than penological. There was a move towards performance management, but concerns about law and order operated more at the level of rhetoric than reality. Probation was disquieted at being manoeuvred into a punishment in the community towards the end of the 1980s, even if this strategic tactic curbed the

DOI: 10.1057/9781137468468.0007

prison population. I distinctly recall being a relatively new probation officer during the 1980s receiving the organisational authority to apply the knowledge and skill acquired at Lancaster University between 1979 and 1981 to function as a *social worker of the court* (Home Office, 1962). No one manipulated my hand to cultivate an iron fist to engage in muscular punitive working practices. It was after 1992 that the politics of punishment began to seep into probation, and the gap narrowed between rhetoric and reality as the expressive pronouncements at conservative party conferences in 1993 and 1995 percolated the organisation. But even this requires qualification by reference to the Two Demonstration Projects. If the political doctrine of conservatism is defined by preserving what is of value from the past, increasingly, between 1979 and 1997, we are confronted with the phenomenon of criminal justice exceptionalism.

As we enter the New Labour dispensation of 1997–2010, there is mounting evidence on the quantity of, and rule by, legislative fiat. New Labour was more preoccupied with expanding the net of criminal justice legislation to govern through crime, than initiating public debate on ethics and justice. The classical Greek understanding of justice (δικαιοσύνη dikaiosunē) that conveyed a more moral than legal meaning was lost on the modernisers. There was continuity, if not expansion, of the neoliberal platform and fiscal deregulation that culminated in the crisis of 2007–08. There was also continuity with the previous surge of expressive retributive punishment, prison and increasing discomfiture with the *what are we going to do about probation* question that ideologically marooned the organisation. Probation was threatened with closer alignment to the prison estate through reducing cultural divides, illustrative of a politics of moral indifference for its distinctive history, culture and working practices as first the Home Office and then Ministry of Justice, from 2007, seized command and exercised control through the National Probation Service and National Offender Management Service. Repositioning probation, criminal justice and penal policy assumed greater importance than reviewing intellectual and moral coordinates that would have provided the opportunity to reevaluate the punitive drift since the early 1990s. Rather than New Labour advancing arguments for an ethico-cultural corrective to the five years before it came to office, it expanded the former period. Intellectual disquiet was exemplified in the punitisation of *enforcement* practices, and moral disquiet at the *benefit sanction*. If I can recall the scope to practice as a social worker of the courts in the 1980s, I do not recall rigorous discussion about the threat being posed to the moral foundations of probation and criminal justice during the 1990s. I remember endless discussions on technical and bureaucratic modalities, the introduction of computers after 2001 and micro managerial processes that entombed probation in a bureaucratic iron cage. But no one sufficiently questioned the ethico-cultural implications for criminal justice if probation officers were relegated to the bureaucratic and punitive technicians of a repressive state apparatus. These were intellectual and moral issues of material import that were not addressed as rigorously as they should have been. The critical question, lingering with residual survivor guilt, is whether those of us inside the organisation could have done something, anything, to resist those radical transformations that carved out a situation of moral vacuity.

We know that criminal justice and penal policy are complex matters, not least because they reflect and reproduce the interests of conflicting constituencies. It is a field replete with contradiction, continuity and discontinuity, differences of degree and kind and where strategic political posturing gets muddled with the objectives of criminal and social justice. The criminal justice system is forged by strategic political alliances, the election cycle, keeping an eye on public and penal appearances, ideological and axiological conviction across a wide spectrum of political, professional and organisational interests. What is deemed politically useful clashes with penal effectiveness, there are always fiscal constraints..., but monies made available to expand the prison estate. Wacquant has argued that there is 'no master-scheme concocted by omniscient rulers. To reiterate the warnings sounded in the book's prologue: the overall fitness of punitive containment to regulate urban marginality at century's dawn is a rough *post-hoc functionality* born of a mix of initial policy intent, sequential bureaucratic adjustment, and political trial-and-error and electoral profit-seeking at the point of confluence of three relatively autonomous streams of public measures concerning the low-skill employment market, public aid and criminal justice' (2009: 312). We also know that years of rebalancing and modernisation have reconfigured the uneasy alliance between care and control, welfare and punishment, rehabilitation, treatment and justice, community and prison, public sector probation, private sector solutions and market driven operations. Critically, attention to moral issues has not kept pace with political, legislative, economic and administrative developments in the criminal justice domain. If this was increasingly evident from 1992 through 1997–2010, it is even more evident in the next chapter.

DOI: 10.1057/9781137468468.0007

Notes

1 Hedges (2010) associates liberal-democratic culture and values with universal human rights, Democratic rather than Republican politics, social democracy, the media, church, universities, arts and labour unions. This culture and representative institutions wanted to 'better humankind' (2010: 84) but has sold out to the narrow vortex of the power elite. Therefore, 'A country that stops taking care of its own, that loses the capacity for empathy and compassion, that crumples up human beings and throws them away when it has done with them, breeds dark ideological monsters that will inevitably rise to devour the body politic' (2010: 191). See also Faulkner (2014); Marquand (2014); Mumford (1940).

2 Salient features of CJA 1991: Probation was awarded the task of delivering punishment in the community; reports continued to address the *what* and *why* questions; community sentences tough and demanding to enhance their credibility to magistrates and judges to reduce prison sentences; the attempt at s29 *not* to make current offences more serious because of previous convictions; punishment to fit the crime and a sentencing philosophy of just deserts. Also, the introduction of three sentencing bands to ensure offences had to be '*serious enough*' to warrant a community sentence, and '*so serious*' that only custody can be imposed. However, ss65 and 66 of CJA 1993 imposed changes to the 1991 Act because of judicial opposition. Specifically, it weakened the position appertaining to previous convictions and response to previous sentences that became aggravating features to the current offences. See discussion in Whitehead and Statham (2006: 136).

3 Hall et al. (1978) advance a *fully social theory of deviance* by referring to the 1970s phenomenon of mugging and moral panic generated by the media that fabricated and amplified rather than 'objectively' reported events. The state was faced with socioeconomic dislocations, a crisis of legitimacy and, it is argued, engendered moral panics to divert attention away from the real source of the problem in class relations and political-economic organisation associated with capitalism. Crime was utilised by the state as a 'symbolic source of unity in an increasingly divided class society at a time when traditional modes of providing consensus were diminishing' (Valier, 2002: 122). A veil of ideological mystification was cast over the 'real' source of the problem which was capitalism. Capitalism was restructured at the expense of the working class; maintain profits for the few; from class conflict to authority relations as crime and politics were separated.

4 *Successes* are enumerated as youth justice reforms, safer and securer prisons, more responsive police, enhanced sensitivity to race and gender, the revival of rehabilitation and clarification to the purposes of sentencing at s142 CJA 2003. *Failures* are too much legislation, NOMS expensive and poorly

DOI: 10.1057/9781137468468.0007

managed, computerisation put probation work at a distance from offenders, New Public Management, business models, privatisation and markets, deprofessionalisation and dehumanisation of services, command and control imposed from the centre through the National Probation Service in 2001 and NOMS 2003, and ethico-cultural erosion at the hands of managerial bureaucracy.

DOI: 10.1057/9781137468468.0007

4

Moral Economy, Markets and Privatisation: From 2010 to 2015

Abstract: *The period for this analysis is primarily from 2010 to 2015. Initially, though, it is necessary to reiterate thematic continuities with previous bouts of privatisation in the 1980s,[1] followed by the National Offender Management Service on contestability. Next, in 2005, the Home Secretary, Charles Clarke, moved in the direction of market testing probation, before the Offender Management Act 2007 normalised competition. Consequently, the first task produces a documentary review from 2008 when the conservative party was in opposition. This review exposes criminal justice transformations to the paradox of frantic activity conducted in moral silence. Second, Payment by Results constitutes a material signifier of reconstruction which provokes moral questions. Third, it is pertinent to embed criminal justice revolutionary activity within a broader historical, politico-economic context.*

Whitehead, Philip. *Reconceptualising the Moral Economy of Criminal Justice: A New Perspective.* Basingstoke: Palgrave Macmillan, 2015. DOI: 10.1057/9781137468468.0008.

Documentary review from 2008 to 2014

In 2008, two years out from the general election, the Conservative Party (2008) published *Prisons with a Purpose*. The document refers to energy supplies, pollution, economic stability, national security, immigration, transport and development, before turning to crime and prisons. Students of criminal justice are inured to consulting the crisis literature on crime, prison overcrowding and longer prison sentences since 1993, reoffending rates,[2] community sentences that lack credibility and the volume of crime committed by offenders with previous convictions. Accordingly, the 'right way to reduce the prison population is to break the cycle of re-offending and reduce crime' (2008: 4). It is imperative to restore confidence in the criminal justice system which will be achieved by launching a rehabilitative revolution in which community and prison sentences reflect four basic principles: punishment, rehabilitation, employment and reparation for victims. Additionally, community sentences must be tough and demanding to enhance their credibility and to improve compliance, which repeats familiar themes. *Prisons with a Purpose* also threatens benefit withdrawal for noncompliance with community sentences, a policy previously introduced and abandoned by New Labour (Whitehead 2010: 116). Furthermore, the crisis in criminal justice is explained by insufficient prison capacity, the imposition of centrally imposed targets that paralysed prison governors and probation officers. In fact, the 'Probation Service in particular has been burdened with too many targets' (2008: 25). This analysis admits to organisational weaknesses but also proffers liberating possibilities after the stultifying, target-driven and bureaucratically obsessed governmental regimes (Whitehead, 2010). However, it is intriguingly stated that 'We want to see new providers brought in to *aid* the probation service ...' (2008: 80).

There is a vestige of hope for probation services after nationalisation in 2001 which established the National Probation Service (NPS), then the National Offender Management Service after 2003, because of the tantalising prospect of energising professional autonomy and discretion. However, a closer reading of the text precipitates a number of niggling concerns: subjecting prison regimes to Payment by Results (PbR, the first of many references in the literature between 2008 and 2014), expanding the role of the voluntary and private sectors and incentivising performance. Some features are new in tone, for example PbR; others continuous with previous developments such as value for money, and the deeper penetration of privatisation and market expansion. However, there are two significant omissions. First, analysis and solutions are not intellectually embedded within an explanatory historical, politico-economic and social context. The document fails to consider political decisions during the previous thirty years, the impact of governmental policies, material conditions leading to the crisis in 2007–08, neoliberal ideology and the moral implications of pursuing fiscal efficiencies. This lacuna distorts the analysis compared to the aforementioned *Review* (Home Office, 1977) cited in chapter three. Second, there is an air of silence on the content of, and arguments for, the moral coordinates of criminal justice and penal policy. Canton (2007: 236; cited in Faulkner and Burnett, 2012: 132) argues that work with offenders is a *morally significant activity* that cannot be reduced to technical gimmicks for achieving efficiency and effectiveness. The dialectic of criminal justice combine fiscal considerations *and* personalist ethics, but *Prisons with a Purpose* is silent on the latter. In 2008 the battle-lines are being sketched and, in May 2010, the conservative party entered coalition with the liberal democrats. By December 2010 a Green Paper was published.

Breaking the Cycle (Ministry of Justice, 2010; see Whitehead, 2011a) is a significant document because it proposes fundamental changes to the criminal justice system to ensure 'improved public safety through more effective punishments that reduce the prospect of criminals reoffending time and time again' (2010: 5). The thematic focus is local solutions for local problems to utilise expertise wherever it can be found, which juxtaposes the Big Society with the Rehabilitation Revolution. *Breaking the Cycle* repeats the refrain that the prison population had doubled since 1993 (but fails to come clean that this followed the decision of a previous conservative administration). Retribution displaced rehabilitation; reconviction rates are too high and costly at £7–10 billion annually; there are 16,000 active offenders at any one time, each with 75 previous convictions. There is also the admission that the weight of criminal legislation since 1997 has been excessive rather than measured. The principles of reform underpinning the Rehabilitation Revolution are public protection, punishment *and* rehabilitation, transparency and accountability and the decentralisation of services. It is creditably acknowledged that crime is committed by offenders with a surfeit of problems, and the proposed reforms offer a once in a generation opportunity to make a difference. There are five substantive sections in the Green Paper.[3] Importantly, PbR is foregrounded as a radical reform that signals the transference of

DOI: 10.1057/9781137468468.0008

financial risks from taxpayers to the new providers. Consequently, there will be a competition strategy to determine the provision of services according to commercial and market principles (see Sandel, 2012 on the transition from a market economy to market society). In other words, the Ministry of Justice will no longer pay for good intentions. Again, silence enshrouds the moral foundations of criminal justice, nor does *Breaking the Cycle* consider the theoretical possibility that services to offenders may have value even though they achieve 'nothing'. Rather than weaving a nomenclature with reference to the good, right, fair, just and the ethical duty of government and criminal justice organisations, the Green Paper foregrounds future business opportunities, commercial interests, and fiscal rewards for achieving reductions in reoffending. At no point is sufficient consideration given to the archaeological deposits, historical traditions, or ethico-cultural contribution of probation work to the system of criminal justice. A narrow-minded and market-orientated perspective invades the criminal justice domain.

Modernising Commissioning (Cabinet Office, 2010) comments on the Rehabilitation Revolution and associated plans for commissioning services through the expansion of mutuals, cooperatives, charities and social enterprises in running public services. At this early stage the coalition government is actively turning towards profit-making businesses with commercial objectives to assume an enhanced role in public service reform. The accumulating documentary evidence provides a strong steer on how public services should be delivered in future: the relentless demands to improve efficiency and effectiveness, investment opportunities, private is superior to public provision, the expansion of markets, and reducing risks to taxpayers through PbR. Accordingly, 'As announced in the Spending Review, the Government intends to identify particular opportunities to expand the use of payment by results across particular services areas' (Cabinet Office, 2010: 9). Nevertheless, *Modernising Commissioning* does not raise moral objections appertaining to the state disposing of its ethico-cultural responsibilities to diverse providers, or the implications for probation. The scythe of privatisation, marketisation and diversification is struck at the moral and cultural fabric of criminal justice.

The following year *Open Public Services* (H.M. Government, 2011) asserted that the reform of public services is a 'key progressive cause' (2011: 5). In doing so it conflated reform with the task of civilising society, but omits the problematic of reconciling the commercial platform with

DOI: 10.1057/9781137468468.0008

the ethical provision of services. In other words, is it possible to create good public services to enhance the social domain if the Symbolic is relegated to the Real, if material priorities consume the ethico-cultural? This document continues the thematic trend of reform through the fiscal mechanism of PbR which is being applied to numerous organisational spheres, including the Work Programme, public health, drug and alcohol recovery services, children's centres, vulnerable people, as well as the rehabilitation revolution in prisons and probation (paragraph 5.14: 33). Five additional principles of reform are cited: increased choice, decentralisation, diversity of providers, fair access to services and accountability to taxpayers. Ideologically, with no supporting evidence, it is stated that 'Our reforms are the best way to deliver better services; indeed, they are the only way we can deliver improved, modern public services in a time of fiscal consolidation and growing demand' (paragraph 1.27: 11).

Next, the *Competition Strategy* (Ministry of Justice, 2011) reinforced the aforementioned documentary themes, confirming that competition in offender services can be traced to 1992 with the first private prison at HMP Wolds (currently 11 private prisons). However, the market in non-custodial sentences is much less developed. Therefore, the Ministry of Justice aspires to build on the platform of competition, inchoate privatisation, the Private Finance Initiative (PFI) prison building programme, better value for money (VfM) in the delivery of prison escort and custody services, bail accommodation and the expansion of electronic monitoring. A competition strategy is required to identify the most suitable providers to deliver offender services which include custodial provision, community services, health, substance misuse and learning skills for offenders. When shifting the focus from custody to the community 'The starting point here is different, as the use of competition in delivering core probation services is less developed, as is the market for providing these services' (Ministry of Justice, 2011: 15). The drivers of public service and criminal justice reform are elucidated as financial rationalisation, VfM, outcomes, target achievement, risk and reward, business models and commercial practices, the diversity of providers, privatisation, markets and competition between the sectors. Again, for comparative purposes, this operating framework is incompatible with the aforementioned *Review* (Home Office, 1977). It is also discernibly different to the 1980s and 1990s, primarily because the nature and scale of reform is more penetrative. The past was a different place, intellectually and morally, compared to the period under consideration here.

DOI: 10.1057/9781137468468.0008

Two significant documents were published in March 2012: *Punishment and Reform: Effective community sentences* (Ministry of Justice, 2012a); *Punishment and Reform: Effective probation services* (Ministry of Justice, 2012b). Previously, *Prisons with a Purpose* in 2008 stated that reconviction rates were too high, indicative of lamentable failure. Now, four years later, this problem will be remedied by allowing probation to retain responsibility for approximately 40,000 high-risk offenders and the production of court reports for magistrates and judges. The remaining low to medium risk offenders, approximately 220,000, will be the subject of market competition between the public, private and voluntary sectors. Consequently, 'The aim of all this is to free up a traditional, old-fashioned system and introduce new ways of operating and delivering that will help drive a reduction in reoffending' (2012a: 3). The accompanying publication, *Effective Probation Services*, extends the principle of competition in the *Offender Management Act 2007*. On reflection, it would have been beneficial to reflect with greater acuity on why the 'modern' is presumed to be superior to established historical traditions; the new superior to the old; competition better than cooperation; private enterprise superior and more efficient than public duty and service. Additionally, there is the problematic of efficiency targets swamping moral questions, and restructuring and rebalancing, unbalancing the dialectics of criminal justice by eroding historical, cultural and ethico-cultural conventions. Finally, also during 2012, the White Paper *Swift and Sure Justice* (Ministry of Justice, 2012c) supported the intellectual justification for reforming the criminal justice system in England and Wales, by repeating the arguments for modernisation of an outdated infrastructure that delivers justice too slowly and costly.

The year 2013 is significant for Transforming Rehabilitation that began in January (Ministry of Justice, 2013b) with a period of consultation until the 22 February. This New Year document provides further detail on the structural mechanisms required to deliver reform, and nineteen questions are posed for consultation that does nothing to reduce the moral vacuity of *Breaking the Cycle*. These questions refer to PbR, the pricing structure and incentives for providers, bureaucracy, incentivising performance, managing poor performance, the supply chain of offender services, integrating the public, private and voluntary sectors, relevant legislation, noncompliance, probation and other delivery systems, maximising local expertise, maintaining professional standards and the role of the Inspectorate. None of these questions initiate reasoned

DOI: 10.1057/9781137468468.0008

discussion and public debate on the intellectual and moral foundations of criminal justice. Subsequently, the Ministry of Justice published its response to the consultation in *Transforming Rehabilitation: A Strategy for Reform* (2013c). First, under the rubric of *Reducing Reoffending*, rehabilitation and mentoring services will be statutorily provided to all offenders including those sentenced to less than 12 months. Consequently, 'Competing services will allow us to use innovative payment mechanisms which drive a focus on reducing reoffending. Providers' level of payment will therefore be dependent on the reductions in reoffending they achieve' (2013c: 14). PbR is elucidated as a mechanism to facilitate fiscal incentives; providers must assist *all* offenders not just those who will 'succeed' which would rig payment in favour of investors' vested interests; providers will be financially rewarded for success when offenders and former prisoners achieve complete desistance for 12 months; payment mechanisms will take account of the total number of offences committed by offenders. Therefore 'The combined payment mechanism, including "fee for service" and "payment by results" elements will mean that providers need to work successfully with all offenders, in order to get paid in full' (2013c: 15). Next, the section on *Protecting the Public* proposes a new public sector probation service after 60–70% of its work has been opened up to competition. Then, *Making the System Work* indicates that some probation staff will transfer into the private and voluntary sectors. This signals the end of probation trusts through the creation of a new NPS managed by the Ministry of Justice and NOMS. By autumn 2014 it is envisaged that there will be 21 Contract Package Areas of diverse providers called Community Rehabilitation Companies (CRCs) to deliver criminal justice services alongside a truncated probation system. Between May 2013 and autumn 2014 potential providers, including large private companies (Interserve, G4S and Sodexo Justice Services), were encouraged to bid for Ministry of Justice contracts.

In September 2013, the Ministry of Justice (2013d) issued the *Target Operating Model* which consolidated the structure to deliver more effective rehabilitative outcomes. It includes through-the-gate services for offenders sentenced to less than 12 months of imprisonment that necessitate new licence arrangements. Furthermore, the reformed structure endorses marketised competition between the sectors, the flexibility to innovate, a new NPS and 21 CRCs. It is specified that payment to the Rehabilitation Companies 'will be based on a weighted annual volume of offender starts, with a proportion of the payment at risk, dependent on their performance in reducing reoffending' (2013d: 5). The NPS will be responsible for writing court reports and sentencing advice to the courts, risk assessment, allocating cases, the management of high-risk cases, enforcement of community orders and licences, Parole Board duties and Multi-Agency Public Protection Arrangements (MAPPA). Accordingly, existing Probation Trusts will be dissolved on the 31 March 2014 and staff allocated to either the NPS or CRC. Nevertheless, a number of concerns were articulated during the transitional phase before the new arrangements were finally determined, which included: the necessity for and pace of reforms, their rationale, making the transitional arrangements work, tender processes, how the market will work and the relationship between NPS and CRC if there is a change in the risk status of offenders, as assuredly there will be, PbR and penalties for failure, the risks and costs of reform, staff retention and potential loss of skills.

Therefore, after much activity between *Breaking the Cycle* of December 2010 and the cumulative events of 2013, 30 bidders passed the first stage of the competition process to win the 21 CRC contracts to lead the new era in a fight against offending (announced on 13 December 2013 in Ministry of Justice, 2013e). The bids were submitted by a mélange of organisations and partnerships who want to lead the rehabilitation revolution, such as private firms, charities, businesses and multinationals. It was anticipated that the successful bidders would be announced during the autumn of 2014. For the Ministry of Justice the rehabilitation revolution exemplifies innovative ways of doing business differently, the best way of using taxpayers' money – the contracts are worth £450 million annually – and, in addition to bids from lead providers, 800 organisations expressed an interest in the delivery supply chain. It should be noted that the proposals for reform were scrutinised by the *House of Commons Justice Committee* (14 January 2014). Some committee members expressed approbation at the direction of travel since 2008, but others concern that reducing the role of the public sector probation service is unconvincing, too risky, untested and unpiloted, and therefore unlikely to deliver better results. Furthermore, there were divergent views from witnesses appearing before the committee. It is acknowledged that there are gaps in current practice, such as support being unavailable to offenders leaving prison after serving less than 12 months (erstwhile prison voluntary aftercare cases – PVAC). Consequently, the evidence presented to the committee during 2013, including Ministry of Justice officials, consolidated the position that Transforming Rehabilitation has four elements:

▶ Extend statutory rehabilitation to those sentenced to less than 12 months – an extra 50,000 offenders
▶ Open up rehabilitation services to a diverse market of providers and new payment mechanisms
▶ Create a new NPS primarily involved in public protection
▶ Reorganise the prison estate

Most of the proposals can be undertaken through the *Offender Management Act 2007*, but new legislation is required to extend supervision to short-term prisoners beginning with the *Offender Rehabilitation Bill*. The Conclusions and Recommendations from the Committee report are enumerated as follows:

▶ Extending statutory supervision for offenders sentenced to 12 months of imprisonment or less is a positive reform
▶ There remain serious questions about the evidence-base for reform–ironic given the emphasis on What Works since 1992
▶ Witnesses expressed apprehension at the pace, scale, architecture, detail and likely consequences of reform
▶ Risks to the system and costs
▶ Retention of skills and the development of staff in the 21 CRCs
▶ PbR is the principle of reward for success and punishment for failure morally acceptable?

'The Ministry has high expectations of what can be achieved in the way of efficiency savings and extension of services through contracting out the management of low and medium risk offenders within existing resources. It seems entirely feasible to us that as the competition progresses and details are refined, the attractiveness of these contracts might wane, resulting in incomplete or inadequate provision in certain areas or types of service' (House of Commons, 2014, paragraph 25 of *Conclusions and Recommendations*).

On Wednesday 29 October, 2014, Chris Grayling, Justice Secretary, announced the decision on the successful bidders for the 21 CRCs: Sodexo Justice Services in partnership with NACRO (6 areas), ARCC (1), Purple Futures (5), The Reducing Reoffending Partnership (2), Working Links (3), Geo Mercia Willowdene (1), MTCNovo (2) and Seetec (1). Fuller details are (but also refer to)[4]:

▶ Northumbria: Sodexo Justice Services in partnership with NACRO
▶ Cumbria and Lancashire: Sodexo Justice Services in partnership with NACRO

▶ Durham and Tees Valley: ARCC
▶ Humberside, Lincolnshire and North Yorkshire: Purple Futures
▶ West Yorkshire: Purple Futures
▶ Cheshire and Greater Manchester: Purple Futures
▶ Merseyside: Purple Futures
▶ South Yorkshire: Sodexo Justice Services in partnership with NACRO
▶ Staffordshire and West Midlands: The Reducing Reoffending Partnership
▶ Derbyshire, Leicestershire, Nottinghamshire and Rutland: The Reducing Reoffending Partnership
▶ Wales: Working Links
▶ Warwickshire and West Mercia: Geo Mercia Willowdene
▶ Bristol, Gloucestershire, Somerset and Wiltshire: Working Links
▶ Dorset, Devon and Cornwall: Working Links
▶ Hampshire and Isle and Wight: Purple Futures
▶ Thames Valley: MTCNovo
▶ Bedfordshire, Northamptonshire, Cambridgeshire and Hertforshire: Sodexo Justice Services in partnership with NACRO
▶ Norfolk and Suffolk: Sodexo Justice Services in partnership with NACRO
▶ Essex: Sodexo Justice Services in partnership with NACRO
▶ London: MTCNovo
▶ Kent, Surrey and Sussex: Seetec

Additional comment on PbR

The documents cited above incorporate frequent references to PbR. Because of its semiotic significance in the new dispensation an additional explanatory comment is required. The first substantive application of PbR to the criminal justice system is the six-year pilot that began in 2010 at HMP Peterborough. This project provides rehabilitation and mentoring services to 3000 offenders serving sentences of less than 12 months which commences in prison and continues beyond release. Peterborough is a Category B establishment operated by Sodexo Justice Services, one of eleven private prisons in England and Wales (also 111 public prisons), that won the contract to run 6 of 21 CRCs. The point for emphasis is that the Ministry of Justice contracted with Social Finance (see its dedicated website) that was established in 2007 to build a social investment market in the United Kingdom. Its rationale is to raise capital to fund social projects according to measures of success and failure determined by market principles. Funds can be raised from a variety of sources including local authorities, private/commercial investors, philanthropists and associated charitable foundations, as well as national lottery funds. The next step was for Social Finance to fund the St. Giles Trust to deliver the intervention to reduce reoffending beyond release, in addition to which the Ormiston Trust provides support to prisoners' families. If the intervention delivers a reduction in reoffending by 7.5% or more then the Social Impact Bond, the outcome-based contract mechanism, results in investors receiving a return of up to 13% of the original investment. The premium will be funded by the Ministry of Justice from anticipated savings accrued in the overall reduction in reoffending (Cabinet Office, 2010). However, if the 7.5% outcome target is not achieved then investors must bear the risks and costs, rather than the taxpayer/treasury. Under PbR the Ministry of Justice only pays for demonstrable and measurable successful outcomes in reducing reoffending. The interim results at Peterborough were encouraging, in fact more encouraging than the Doncaster pilot (Ministry of Justice, 2013f). But what about offenders sentenced to community supervision? Although, as explained earlier, the probation service will retain responsibility for offenders on community orders and prison licences who present a serious risk of harm to the public, most community-based services will be delivered by the 21 CRCs to low and medium risk offenders. These services, locked into the parameters of the internal market by political fiat, will deliver accommodation; mentoring; employment, training and education; alcohol and drug addiction support; and supervising community orders and appropriate low risk prison licences. They will also be subjected to PbR. For further information: see Chambers (2013) on the case for expanding PbR; Knight-Markiegi and Quinn (2013) compare the implementation of PbR across public services; also, Whitehead (2015). Finally, in addition to open source material, one should also refer to associated websites, tweets and blogs: Russell Webster [http://www.russellwebster.com] on what is quickly becoming a discrete industry of the new organisational orthodoxy. If the documents from 2008 make repeated references to the new funding mechanism, by contrast they omit to locate developments in criminal justice within a broader historical and political context which should be remedied.

DOI: 10.1057/9781137468468.0008

Historical and contemporary embedding

Since the breakthrough of the capitalist system towards the end of the 1700s in England, it has survived periodic crises of varying intensity (Hobsbawm, 1977; 1994). By the early 19th century it was plain that liberalism inflicted socioeconomic dislocations, but ethico-cultural objections were not sufficient to curb its depredations. A century later, notwithstanding the ameliorative social legislation of the reforming Liberal government between 1906 and 1914, the 1920s and 1930s were economically catastrophic, the predictable outcome of capitalist logic (Varoufakis, 2013). Contrastingly, the golden age interregnum between 1950 and the 1970s with its mixed economy, stability, economic growth and policy of full employment that characterised the Keynesian 'solidarity project' (Garland, 2001; Marquand, 2014) established the National Health Service, consolidated educational and welfare reforms and expanded the social security safety net to offer protection against the vagaries of the capitalist order. The organisational structures that delivered health, education and welfare services were integrated into the solidarity project, as the post-war consensus established a new social contract between capital and labour. For approximately 30 years, first under Atlee, then Butskellism, the principle of 'moderate dirigisme' (Lawson, 2013) prevailed. The criminal justice system, located alongside other organisational structures of the post-war settlement, was orientated towards rehabilitation not punitive retribution, thus constituting a logical adjunct to the integrative and solidifying objectives of the social democratic state in response to the perennial threat of social disorder. Importantly, criminal justice, and those organisations delivering health, education and welfare, were supported by the state and funded out of general taxation to facilitate the good society. Accordingly, social democracy and its load-bearing organisational pillars reflected and reproduced a governmental rationality, including a set of axiological signifiers of social value, in marked contrast to 19th century Victorian liberalism.

By 1979 the post-war consensus and one-nation conservatism were assailed by a brand of radical–liberal conservatism which argued that, because of the growing economic problems during the 1970s – recession, inflation, industrial disputes, unemployment and public spending out of control – post-war social democracy had failed. Keynesian polity was unravelled by economic dislocations, manifested in economic insecurity which culminated in the demise of social democracy (it was Callaghan's

DOI: 10.1057/9781137468468.0008

speech to the Labour conference in 1976 that signalled the end of the Keynesian economic policy that governments should spend their way out of recession; see Skidelsky, 2003: 846). According to Lord Lawson's analysis of the Thatcher decade, the Keynesian modality which advocated a managed and interventionist economy was rejected precisely because it had demonstrably 'failed'. He acknowledges in his encomium of Thatcherism that no economic system is perfect, so that 'all we can sensibly do is to put in place a system in which mistakes are soonest recognised and most rapidly corrected. And this means, in practice, the *liberal capitalist market economy*' (2013, 13 italics added). In other words, it was acceptable to replace the social democratic nation state with the market state (Bobbitt, 2002). Lawson's analysis, understandably supportive of the government he served, is intellectually questionable in its advocacy of liberal market capitalism. First, the accumulated evidence of the last 200 years in the United Kingdom and United States cogently illustrates that liberal capitalism, as well as providing material benefits for the few, correspondingly inflicts periodic crises and social damage on the many (Harvey, 2010). Second, this is the system with its neoliberal variant since the 1980s under successive conservative administrations, followed by New Labour governments between 1997 and 2010 and the coalition government after 2010, that benefited economic elites as the restoration of profit was actively pursued in a deregulated economy. Third, this is the system that culminated in the economic crisis of 2007–08 which Lord Lawson argues was not caused by previous conservative governments because the 1987 Banking Act strengthened regulation. Deft political footwork allows him to load the blame for economic malfeasance on the Blair/Brown governments for undermining these regulations and liberating dysfunctionality into the system. However, the Big Bang of October 1986 deregulated financial markets and weakened restraint through unlimited leverage and risk, which were contributory factors of the latest crisis. He tries to wriggle off what is a compelling evidential hook by claiming that what occurred in 2007–08 was an *unintended* consequence of the Big Bang, that the Blair/Brown axis exacerbated by further deregulation in pursuit of bonuses before the public interest. Finally, and paradoxically, this is the system which is being reconstructed rather than abandoned during 2010–15, but this time more intensively by exposing almost everything to market forces (Sandel, 2012), which situates the analysis of PbR and attendant probation reforms as key empirical indicators of this reconstruction. The perverted logic being applied

DOI: 10.1057/9781137468468.0008

is that although liberal capitalism has repeatedly benefited the few at the expense of the many, its operating system periodically inflicting socioeconomic crises of varying intensity, in addition to its questionable ethico-cultural effects, future success depends upon *accentuating* rather than attenuating its scope. Just as the faithful will always believe in God regardless of competing perspectives, counter arguments and the slow death of a thousand qualifications, equally there is an unshakable belief in the capitalist order regardless of its catastrophic effects.

Numerous analyses since the 1980s in the United Kingdom and the United States comment upon the re-energising of 19th century economic liberalism (Clarke, 2004: 379). The priorities for the 1979 conservative government were a strong state, the rule of law, sound money and financial discipline, free markets, control over public expenditure, lower taxation and patriotism blended with a dash of populism. Concomitantly faith in capitalist markets after decades of social democratic controls with its nationalised and publicly owned industries precipitated numerous privatisations, enumerated earlier. These privatisations were embedded within and stimulated by neoliberal ideology that has five main features: the privatisation of state assets; liberalisation of trade; monetarism and the control of inflation; the deregulation of labour; marketisation, competition, public–private partnerships and commodification. Crouch (2011: 167) explains that since the 1980s social institutions have been transformed into behaving like business enterprises through commercial practices, business mentalities, and marketised competition, exalting the price mechanism over public service. This process has been psychoanalytically explained as the emancipation of the capital–libidinal drive (Hall, 2012) which has stimulated an anomic free for all, a culture of excessive risk taking, putting profit over people (Chomsky, 1999).

Whitfield's analysis (2012; see also De Angelis, 2007: 89) constructs three schematic subperiods of reform pertinent to this monograph:

1 1980s' neoliberal free markets, financial deregulation and the initial wave of privatisations of utilities.

2 Early 1990s and the escalation of competition and commodification, in addition to the spread of markets in public services.

3 Early 2000s and the consolidation of markets in public services, commissioning, contestability and the hollowing out of the social–public realm. Significantly, and disturbingly for old labour

socialists, New Labour proceeded to create markets in public services that went beyond conservative incursions during the 1980s and early 1990s (Whitfield, 2006).

4 This tripartite schema can be updated by adding a fourth phase from 2010 to 2015 which constitutes the qualitatively deeper immersion of organisations into the circuits of capital concentration and market expansion, and the corresponding erosion of the circuits of ethico-cultural contestation. This qualitative shift signals the transformation of the state from the provider of public services to the animated facilitator of market solutions (Bell, 2011); from the post-war Keynesian social–public state to the neoliberal, commercialised, marketised and privatised state. This transformation is driven forward by a number of features, three of which are emphasised here.

Globalisation: Standing (2011; see also McMurtry, 2002) argues that 1975 to 2008 was the period of globalisation 'when the economy was disembedded from society as financiers and neoliberal economists sought to create a global market economy based on competition and individualism' (2011:26). Furthermore, disembedding the economic from the socio-ethical is proceeding to the next stage of development from a market economy to a market-driven society (Sandel, 2012). This is the process that is facilitating organisational transformations in the interests of capital reconstruction, euphemistically called fiscal consolidation.

State ideology of anti-public service rhetoric: gathered pace under successive conservative administrations after 1979, consolidated by the Major government between 1992 and 1997 through the PFI, followed by New Labour administrations after 1997 (Whitfield, 2006; 2012). This ideology is packaged through the claim that the private sector is more effective and efficient than the public sector with its outmoded practices and poor management, exemplified by the Rehabilitation Revolution. Moreover, this ideology transforms organisations from turning outward in pursuit of the common good, to turning inward to ensure economic survival in a market-driven environment. It is a highly questionable strategy to have faith in the beneficial effects of private finance and the rationality of markets, an observation made by the House of Commons Justice Committee (2014) cited earlier. In support of Sandel's (2012) analysis, Marquand asserts that marketisation is a 'process of rhetorical and behavioural colonisation that intruded market norms and market

DOI: 10.1057/9781137468468.0008

practices into the public realm' (2014: 109). The probation ideal, rehabilitative ethic, public duty and service, utilising the social work skills of a professional class do not fit with this platform – a platform at worst a-moral and at best indifferent to the moral, cultural and professional conventions of the probation system rooted in the personal social services under the welfare–social dispensation.

Austerity and debt management after 2007–08: should be evaluated as a consequence of the deregulated 1980s and 1990s when the City of London wrested greater control over economic life, remaking the country in its own image. Therefore, by 2008 the banking sector had lost regulatory control over its own domain because of irresponsible financial practices, playing by their own rules rather than complying with the symbolic order of the now defunct Financial Services Authority (renamed as the Financial Conduct Authority). What is more the failure of the capitalist order became culturally endemic, manifested in the primacy attached to business, the salience of profit making and the escalation of financial interests above all others. Lanchester, in his populist account, states that 'Regulation, and the lack of it, and the slack enforcement of it, was central to the crunch' (2010: 155; see also Varoufakis, 2013). Additionally, 'Austerity aims at rearranging late capitalism in conditions of severe crisis. The contraction of the state through "fiscal discipline" is only part of a wider project affecting every part of society' (Douzinas, 2013: 11). From the analysis of Douzinas in Greece to organisational reconstruction in England and Wales, it seems that almost everything is being reconfigured in the interests of capital markets.[5]

The reconfiguration of organisational structures contingent upon the deeper penetration of neoliberal–capitalist reconstruction between 2010 and 2015 should be situated within a historical trajectory that has evolved over the last few decades. This latest episode is animatedly at work establishing a new platform of which PbR is a significant empirical indicator. This is the platform upon which the transformation of former state supported organisations is occurring, reflecting and reproducing dominant ideological and material interests. In doing so it conforms to its own operating logic, whilst producing irrational ethico-cultural effects to which the system is morally indifferent. This reconfiguration of what were once the state's public sector organisational institutions is a manifestation of capitalist longevity and, as Whitfield explains, the state is now 'primarily dealing and negotiating with private capital through contracts, markets, and regulatory frameworks' (2012: 13). This

DOI: 10.1057/9781137468468.0008

is affecting criminal justice and other organisational domains as 'Public service principles and values are replaced by commercial values and business practices' (Whitfield, 2012: 30). The end result of the transformation from Keynesian social democracy to the neoliberal state is a 'tense, febrile society, in which the past is not just a foreign country, but an inconceivably distant one' (Marquand, 2014: 65). This analysis can be enriched by returning to the Lacanian–Žižekian conceptual framework (see Chapter 1) which has explanatory cogency.

The Lacanian–Žižekian conceptual framework can be extrapolated to advance an analysis of organisational functions shunted onto the PbR material platform, specifically the demise of probation's influence by the imposition of 21 CRCs. De Angelis reminds us that the essence of the capitalist system is market expansion, which has become nothing less than a 'social force that *aspires* to colonise the whole of life practices' (2007: 43; Sandel, 2012 make the same point). Between 2010 and 2015 those organisations previously positioned within, and sustained by, the Keynesian post-war settlement are being materially and ideologically transformed by the logic of market expansion. The acute paradox is that the forces that unleashed the economic turmoil of 2007–08, and previous economic eruptions, proceed with greater penetrative ferocity as they enter organisational domains where previously they had no support. The capitalist Real of exchange relations, the stimulation of competitive desire, narcissistic self-promotion, marketisation and unfettered consumerism, inflict damage upon Symbolic ethics. The canker of the Real is released into the criminal justice system, cogently illustrated in probation, which signals the decline of symbolic efficiency as it is compelled to compete with its competitors in a market–driven environment, vying for fiscal resources and basic economic survival, rather than pursuing the substantive value of personal social service and responding to social need as an honourable public duty. A new operational dispensation replaces the old as the Real genetically modifies organisational rationale, primary tasks and value that corrupt the reproductive mechanisms of the moral. Under cover of austerity the state reduces its ethico-cultural responsibility for public organisations and their ethico-cultural function, to the demand of fiscal constraint and market solutions. Furthermore, the crisis of capitalism that erupted in 2007–08 is far from being wasted. The logical deduction, informed by historical analysis (Piketty, 2014), is that the capitalist system has failed by revealing its inherent flaws and should therefore be replaced. Illogically, and perversely, the system is expanding

DOI: 10.1057/9781137468468.0008

and penetrating in a predatory manner into criminal justice and other organisational domains. The spirit of capitalism is free to roam at will, where it will, recreating organisational life in its own image. Confronted with this evidence, a case can be advanced to reanimate intellectual and moral debate, energised by the conceptual device of moral economy.

Second summation: the moral and political in criminal justice

The previous chapter sequentially plotted intellectual and moral trans-formations in the criminal justice system, strained through filters that included legislative expansion especially after 1997; the political imposi-tion of administrative, managerial and bureaucratic mechanisms of central control; the platform of neoliberal capitalism morally indifferent to punishment and prison; and the recalibration of public–private interests. These accoutrements of a new political order eroded former conventions of the social and penal welfare state. Nowhere is this more clearly delineated than probation. Nevertheless, when turning to assimilate the intellectual disciplines assembled in Chapter 1, and refinements advanced in Chapter 2, we take possession of relevant resources to re-energise the moral. Socrates, preoccupied with ethics and justice, questioned how human beings should conduct their lives. The flourishing life, where human potential is realised, conforms to the virtues (αρέτη aretē) of wisdom and prudence. It is also the examined life that eschews moral complacency and it can never be right, in any circumstances, to harm others. Plato's conception of justice (δικαιοσύνη dikaiosunē) conveyed a moral more than legal meaning. It is broader in scope than the English rendition by combining individual *and* social morality which forges an indissoluble association between ethics and politics. The domain of politics is the domain of ethics and vice versa (see Blumenfeld, 2001), and criminal justice is an absurdity unless it reflects both. Aristotle's εὐδαιμονια (eudaimonia) attends to a 'permanent condition of life or disposition of character, something between prosperity and integration of personality, though of course feeling is involved too' (see Plato, 1974: 101). The good life accords to the human excellences of wisdom, intelligence, prudence, liberality and temperance. Significantly, virtue is the *mean* between excess and deficiency.

Applying the Aristotelian *mean test* to the political reconstruc-tion of criminal justice, including governmental interventions that have violated probation, evidences state inflicted excess rather than the virtuous mean. A gentler and more respectful touch would have sufficed that worked with, not against, the organisation. Excess is the deeper penetration of retributive punishment, manifested in doubling the prison population in England and Wales from 40,000 in 1980 to over 80,000 twenty years later (May 2015:85,704). There were legislative, administrative and bureaucratic excesses under New Labour (see Conservative Party, 2008). Criminal justice has been realigned on the platform of excessive privatisation and marketisation. Of course, there are clear differences between the mental conceptions of classical Greece and the early 21st century. However, Socrates on ethics and virtue, Plato on justice, and Aristotle's eudaimonia, discussed the politico-ethical foundations of the city state, the nature and character of human life in the polis, which are pertinent for theorising morality and justice. Engagement with the rich store of ethical resources of the Western philosophical tradition is urgently required to question and raise issues that are fundamental to the foundations of criminal justice which have been neglected for far too long.

Schweitzer (1929) at a critical juncture in Western European history asserted reverence for life as the basic principle of the moral. This resonates with the Judaeo-Christian tradition, Pauline theologico-political ethics and personalism. These resources are further enriched by Symbolic ethics and Kantian deontology, of which the latter prioritises motive and good will before pseudo-scientific utilitarian calculation. It should not be beyond our collective imagination to conceptualise that some actions – individual, social, organisational – are good and right in themselves. In other words, they may achieve *nothing* according to the criteria of the Rehabilitation Revolution, 3Es, VfM and measurable targets. But this does not invalidate the intrinsic moral value of public duty and service transcending market operations. Nevertheless, ethico-cultural value has been subjected to extreme trans-valuation since the 1980s, especially after 1992. Practical reason suggests that the criminal justice system requires a moral sense (Shaftesbury and Hutcheson) when responding to offending behaviour that inflicts harm on others. It should also be activated in response to excessive punishment that exacerbate rather than ameliorate offenders' lives. Moral sense questions the motives for modernisation, rebalancing and rehabilitation revolution. Hume, influenced by, but proceeding beyond Hutcheson, advanced *feeling* over Enlightenment reason. Hume, the epistemological skeptic,

DOI: 10.1057/9781137468468.0008

dislodges reason to make room for feeling because it is how we feel about an action that determines whether we respond with moral approval or disapproval. This depends upon whether actions produce pleasant or unpleasant outcomes. The law which explains moral feelings is that 'they are caused by acts which either help or hinder human happiness' (1777/1983: 7 Introduction). Accordingly, practical reason, as in cognitive ability and intellectual curiosity, human feeling and empathy, are the constitutive elements of *relationships* in the people-facing professions. They are good in themselves and effective at reducing reoffending as the evidence 'indicates that the relationship between an offender and the person managing them is an important factor in successful rehabilitation' (Ministry of Justice, 2010: 24). This primary human and personalist feature is inadequately considered in the documents of 2008–14, indicative of probation convulsions.

Adam Smith, a devotee of laissez faire and self-interest, endorsed the social passions of generosity, kindness, compassion and the virtues of prudence, justice (do not harm) and beneficence. These are the passions and virtues relegated to inconsequential status by the revolutionary modernisers. Their absence, which has erected a wall of moral silence, throws the whole system out of kilter. The intellectual and moral resources in Chapters 1 and 2 confront the criminal justice system since 1979 in Chapters 3 and 4 with questions of a moral nature that must be urgently confronted. Indubitably, we have the intellectual disciplines and ethico-cultural resources to theorise the moral and reconceptualise moral economy. Additionally, these intellectual and moral resources can re-energise criminal and social justice, probation and penal policy. The dominant storyline since the 1980s recounts modernising and rebalancing reforms, but the subtext is a seeping miasma of moral silence. This has created a moral vacuum into which has rushed a politics of excess, organisational recalibration, exemplified by the disavowal of probation as passé.

Notes

1   British Telecom 1984, British Gas 1986, British Airways 1987, British Petroleum 1979–87, British Aerospace 1985–87, Rolls Royce 1987, British Leyland-Rover 1988, and British Steel 1988.

2   Home Office (2007) publication where two year reconviction rates data controlled for offender characteristics: prison 64.7%, community rehabilitation

order 56.9%, drug treatment and testing order 82.3%, community punishment order 37.9%, community punishment and rehabilitation order 52.2%. See also McNeil and Weaver (2010); Ministry of Justice (2013a) which is a summary of evidence on reducing reoffending.

3   It is stated that 'The Green Paper provides a once in a generation opportunity for new providers from all sectors to work alongside staff in the criminal justice system to make a real difference' (9). The five substantive sections are: (1) Punishment and Payback, (2) Rehabilitate Offenders to Reduce Crime, (3) Payment by Results, (4) Reform Sentencing and (5) Youth Justice. At p. 24 we read that 'Evidence indicates that the *relationship* between an offender and the person managing them is an important factor in successful rehabilitation'.

4   *Sodexo Justice Services*: http://uk.sodexo.com/uken/services/on-site/justice-services/ is in partnership with NACRO in 6 areas. Formerly Kalyx, Sodexo has been running justice services since 1993 in 120 sites across the world, including five prisons in the UK (Peterborough, Northumberland, Forest Bank, Bronzfield and Addiewell). Its values are safety, dignity and opportunity, in addition to which 'Everyone has the right to be treated humanely, decently, respectfully and fairly':

ARCC: http://www.stockton.gov.uk/communitysafety/arcc/ *Achieving Real Change for Communities* is comprised of eight partners and is a not-for-profit organisation to deliver quality services in the North-East of England. At a Conference at Police Headquarters, Ladgate Lane, on 25 January 2014 for the VCE sector, ARCC was confirmed as one of 13 local bidders. ARCC is in partnership with Fabrick Housing, the Wise Group, Safe in Tees Valley, Tees Esk and Wear Valleys Foundation Trust, the Vardy Foundation, Changing Lives in the North East CIC, Stockton Borough Council and Darlington Borough Council.

Purple Futures, an Interserve-led partnership: http://purplefutures.sites.interserve.com/ where staff will be managed by Interserve on behalf of Purple Futures to provide rehabilitative services in conjunction with voluntary groups. Interserve, the majority partner, is 'one of the world's foremost support services and construction companies operating in the UK and internationally'. In 2011 it created a justice team to respond to the emerging Transforming Rehabilitation agenda to deliver a 'Theory of Change' model. It is listed on FTSE 250 Index with gross revenue of £ 3.4 billion and a workforce of over 80,000 worldwide.

The Reducing Reoffending Partnership: http://rrpartnership.com/ is described as a 'ground-breaking new partnership' between Ingeus (work programme), CRI (health and social care charity) and St Giles Trust (work with offenders), combining experience from voluntary and private sectors to deliver the government's Rehabilitation Revolution agenda.

Working Links: http://www.workinglinks.co.uk/ Providing services to people to create better futures.

DOI: 10.1057/9781137468468.0008

Geo Mercia Willowdene: http://geomerciawillowdene.co.uk/ A partnership between the Geo Group Ltd, Mercia Community Action Ltd and Willowdene Rehabilitation Ltd. The Geo group provides custody, detainee transport and offender management across the world (US, UK, South Africa and Australia).

MTC NOVO: http://www.londoncrc.org.uk/news/ seeks to embody the best of probation in a joint innovative venture that embodies the third, public and private sectors to provide rehabilitation services.

Seetec: http://www.seetec.co.uk/ has, since 1984, grown to be one of the UKs largest and most experienced provider of government funded Welfare to Work and skills training programmes. It is expected that the new arrangements will be established by February 2015.

5   This comment requires qualification following a conversation with a former senior probation manager in the North-East on 21 October 2014 at police headquarters, Ladgate Lane. He questioned the material explanation in its application to probation after numerous meetings with NOMS officials. His analysis is that the reforms are more politically and ideologically driven than overtly fiscal to reduce costs. The reforms are unlikely to reduce expenditure due to funding the NOMS managerial hierarchy.

DOI: 10.1057/9781137468468.0008

5
Morality and Justice: Challenging the Established Order

Abstract: *The final chapter returns to motifs that channel their way through preceding chapters, particularly moral economy, criminal justice, probation and penality. The past was a different place before the 1980s, supported by different politico-economic, intellectual and moral conventions. Since the 1980s, and gathering pace towards 2015, hegemonic a-moral neoliberalism has extended the reach of privatisation and market competition into all areas of social life. This has redefined the politico-economic and organisational structures of existence, in addition to subjective experience. Moral economy contains the resources to mount an intellectual and moral challenge to the established order of things.*

Whitehead, Philip. *Reconceptualising the Moral Economy of Criminal Justice: A New Perspective.* Basingstoke: Palgrave Macmillan, 2015. DOI: 10.1057/9781137468468.0009.

It is timely and urgent to engage in a professional and public debate about the criminal justice system in England and Wales. After the punitive turn in 1992–93; the torments endured by probation; the parade of the conjuring modernisers' rebalancing acts that culminated in the rehabilitation revolution; there are serious issues demanding a response. A reconceptualised moral economy facilitates critical engagement with politics, ethics and justice, to restore its position in the dialectical mix where it belongs. Moral economy breaks cover to disturb the moral atrophy recounted in Chapters 3 and 4, to detonate the system out of its slumber of moral indifference. The encroachment of retributive punishment, the lure of the prison (Ministry of Justice, 2013g), the enforced collapse of probation, private interest muscling out public duty, the march of the marketeers, Payment by Results, are all moral issues of pressing seriousness. Any organisation that works with people in health, education and welfare, including that which responds to offenders *in extremis*, is confronted with the task of formulating its moral conventions. If Socrates, Plato and Aristotle were preoccupied with virtue, justice and ethics, this applies equally to criminal justice. The politics of imposition and disavowal over recent decades has reflected insufficiently on these fundamental issues. This is count one on the indictment directed at conservative, labour and coalition governments who are responsible for creating a situation of injudicious amoral deficiency.

Moral economy can be put to work to illuminate moral failings within the criminal justice system, contingent upon the serial assaults made by successive governments on probation. Probation, through the aforementioned rehabilitative ideal and ethic, represented a discernible set of personalist values that informed criminal and social justice. The situation was never perfect (Box, 1987), the supposed Golden Age (Statham, 2014) of the 1960s and 1970s was tarnished by a kind of bronze age since the 1980s. Consequently, *'The past was unlike the present not only in superficial material terms, but morally and intellectually. They did things differently then, and thought and felt differently'* (Burrow, 2009: 115). In addition to exposing a recent history of neglect through punitive excess and moral deficiency, moral economy provides the intellectual resources to re-energise ethical questions, to disturb a post-politics which has rent asunder the relationship between ethics, politics and justice. Moral economy clamours for a hearing to shake the system out of its lethargy, to transcend the crowded market place to engage with ethics and justice that are the requisites of legitimation. Moral economy asks questions of

DOI: 10.1057/9781137468468.0009

all forms of organisational modernisation and revolutionary agendas that outpace moral regulation. The *turn of events* since the 1980s present to those of us who worked in the criminal justice system; those who remain in the reconstituted National Probation Service and newly formed Community Rehabilitation Companies; including those who reflect from a distance – the retired, practitioners turned academics – with a problem. The *turn of events* has turned into the *great problematic* which is to re-energise the content of, and argument for, the moral on what is an expanding neoliberal platform of moral indifference. We must explore this in greater detail.

First, it is cogently argued that *postmodernism* is the cultural logic of late-capitalism (Jameson, 1991). Postmodernism constitutes a modality of existence characterised by radical doubt and where the ethico-cultural is left behind by dominant material interests. It is defined by fragmentation, ontological insecurity, the relative and contingent nature of human experience. In Lacanian and Žižekian terminology it is the collapse of the Big Other. In other words, postmodern culture manifests, reflects and reproduces the politico-economic contours of post-industrial, post-Fordist, consumer capitalism. Second, this analysis is not confined to the cultural trope of postmodernism because human *subjectivity* reflects and reproduces the hegemonic ideological and material signifiers of global capitalism (Hall, 2012; Winlow and Hall, 2013). Alluding to Hegel, MacIntyre captures the point well when stating that 'What passions and what ends the individual has and can have are a matter of the kind of social structure in which the individual finds himself. Desires are elicited and specified by the objects presented to them' (1967: 200). Furthermore, and third, transformations imposed on the criminal justice system reflect and reproduce neoliberal polity. Taking its inspiration from Adam Smith (note the qualifying corrective of moral sentiments), 19th century economic liberalism, the severe economic crises of the 1920s and 1930s, the intellectual supports of Hayek and Friedman, latterly enriched by the neoliberal surge, the capitalist fortress seems unassailable (see Jones, 2015). The doctrine of laissez-faire, competition, individual freedom and responsibility, privatisation, marketisation and the exaltation of moral autonomy over moral economy have combined to create the conditions of existence to exfoliate the moral interest. This is exemplified in the single case study of criminal justice where the identifiable features of neoliberal polity have glacially gouged their way through the system to remake it in its image. The neoliberal order of things has produced conditions of

DOI: 10.1057/9781137468468.0009

advanced marginality, to which the state has responded by penal severity to secure conformity (Bell, 2011; Squires and Lea, 2013; Wacquant, 2009). This, in turn, has demoralised criminal justice and probation is a major casualty as it does not fit with, or belong to, the neoliberal dispensation. It is deduced that 'this liberal economics aims at no more and no less than the domestication of ethics by economics' (Küng, 1998: 192). This is not the result of an inevitable historical process, nor does it conform to the latest phase in the unfolding of a Hegelian master plan. It is not a force of nature determined by the laws of economics to erupt at this precise historical juncture. Things do not have to be the way they are because this is the way they are. Rather, what we have is a consequence of political mis-judgement and injudicious decision-making shaped by the coordinates of neoliberal capitalism. Let us persist with Küng a little longer.

Küng advocates a global ethic in response to a global capitalist order. But there's a problem, not with his analysis but prescription. In the 1990s, some years after the slide of Keynesian social democracy and a decade before the great crash of 2007–08 that rivalled the 1930s in its intensity, he argued for the reunification of ethics and politics. His global ethic is 'none other than the necessary minimum of common human values, criteria and basic attitudes' (1998: 92). In the Küngian universalist universe every human being must be treated humanely, and what you wish for make sure you can reciprocate. It is an ethico-cultural vision of fundamental norms transcending the ephemeral politics of contingency and manipulation. It is a captivating, theologically inspired, humane vision, but it unravels under the weight of a basic flaw. He does not consider, rigorously enough, how a global ethic can be grafted onto an incompatible politico-economic platform that unashamedly prioritises economics before ethics. How is it possible, as a matter of logic, to institute a global ethic, or moral economy, when neoliberal capitalism is premised on exchange relations, the stimulation of desire that induces anthropological anxiety, the release of libidinal energies, destructive drives, fearful competition, the material objects of fixation and material signifiers of self-interest? In the perverted dispensation of the present, the capitalist teleological ethic is quite content to allow innocent taxpayers to foot the bill for the malfeasance of the masters of the universe who were found out again in 2007. It is content to live with austerity, poverty, inequality and injustice that damage all of us, whilst a financial elite continue to prosper (Žižek, 2014). Moral economy and neoliberal

DOI: 10.1057/9781137468468.0009

capitalist political economy represent two different ways of life, conditions of existence, operational circuits and modes of reproduction of human existence.

Looking back, the welfare-orientated Children and Young Person's Act, 1969, could not be grafted onto the politico-economic platform following the general election in June 1970. More recently, the Big Society could not be supported by the politico-economic platform. Since May 2010 the coalition government has aimed to make it 'easier for people to come together to improve their communities and help one another' (HM Government, 2010b: 29). It advocates localism, enhancing communities through voluntary action, the development of a national citizen service, cooperatives, mutuals and charities, and a Big Society bank to fund social investment projects from the proceeds of dormant accounts. At first view its appeal is laudable and plausible, and should not pose insurmountable difficulties when considering the merits of a concept which has acquired thematic relevance. Therefore, there is a prima facie case that the Big Society is replete with good intentions to bolster the social which is 'another name for agreeing and sharing' (Bauman, 2001: 2). However, if we excavate below surface appearances the Big Society is articulated concurrently with the expansion and deeper penetration of the revivified capitalist system following the economic dislocations of 2007–08 (Harvey, 2010; Varoufakis, 2013). A preliminary scan of the politico-economic and ethico-cultural terrain expose a discordant notation because, first, the Big Society appeals to the public–social interest through helping one another; it resonates more with a moral economy than a resurgent liberal political economy; it also requires a human subject who is willing to put others before self-interest. By contrast, capitalist reconstruction is premised upon a discernibly different ideological and material platform: it is more blessed to receive than to give at the expense of the other; atomistic individualism before altruism; profit before people; an ontology of the subject that reflects and reproduces the exigencies of the capitalist system with its exploitative exchange relations; and it advances capital accumulation and market expansion over a moral economy of ethico-cultural social relations. Behind first impressions is a radical disjuncture between the Big Society and resurgent capital.

Extrapolated to criminal justice, the former reproductive mechanisms of symbolic efficiency – the probation ideal, rehabilitative ethic, personalism, inclusive citizenship, relationships of aetiological understanding, an aversion to retributive punishment and prison – have been

DOI: 10.1057/9781137468468.0009

interrupted by exposure to a-moral market forces of which Payment by Results is the master material signifier. The collapse of former conventions through the relentless strafing of probation, has jettisoned criminal justice into the clutches of the capitalist Real. In other words, criminal justice conventions have been displaced by the dictates of the market state. According to Bobbitt (2002) the market state relies upon capital markets, business networks, commercial transactions and investment opportunities to create fiscal stability. Significantly for this monograph, Bobbitt argues that unlike the Keynesian social democratic nation state, the market state is indifferent to justice, ethics, culture and the formulation of universal moral principles. In fact, 'The sense of a single polity, held together by adherence to fundamental values, is not a sense that is cultivated by the market state' (2002: 230). There is little sense of a foundational value beyond the narrow material interest that has reconfigured the criminal justice domain. Küng does not appear to appreciate fully this inherent problem that is a treacherous swamp to negotiate. He wants to ameliorate global capitalism by applying a dose of ethics, but they are incompatible universes of interest. So the system is immured in a deeply problematical situation and I fear corralled into despondency from which there is no illuminated exit sign.

But we are confronted with an existential moral choice, even if we don't exercise it. Either we leave things as they are, do nothing, surrender any hope of formulating an intellectual and moral response to those events recounted in Chapters 3 and 4; or we can begin by reading ourselves into absorbing the lessons that historical analysis teaches. If we boldly select the latter option there are recognisable artifacts of encouragement, scattered deposits of hope, even after the *great transformation* of the 1780s and the pseudo-pacification process (Hall, 2012). The ideological and material contours of 19th century liberalism became untenable by the 1880s that culminated in the reforming liberal government of 1906–14. However, progressive reform was consumed by the catastrophic reverses of the 1920s and 1930s (Whitehead and Crawshaw, 2012). Moreover, the Keynesian social democratic consensus and supporting cast of social-welfare organisations made a difference to people's lives from the 1940s to the 1970s, before being called into question by the Callaghan labour government of 1976 to 1979 (Stewart, 2013). In the thematic context of this monograph there has never been a fully functioning, permanently installed, and universally accepted moral economy. It is persistently up against it and the present situation is indubitably difficult. But this does not mean that there is no scope to advance the content of, and arguments for, the moral interest in the criminal justice system. It is true that current circumstances are intellectually and morally less favourable than they were, and to plot an alternative future is of Odyssean complexity because of the uncertainties and frustrations that block our path. A recent history of repeated onslaughts from above is not a propitious basis upon which to initiate a change of direction from below. Who cares about the ethics of criminal justice anyway? The Big Other has collapsed; the sources of symbolic efficiency declined; we operate in a moral void. Although *little others* have emerged to fill the gap, they do not possess the authority of the Big Other and seem destined to fail[1]. Organisations find themselves in circumstances not of their choosing, dealt a hand they neither pursued not wanted, but criminal justice has its modest little others to compensate for the loss of probation's symbolic efficiency. Accordingly, if a case can be made to reestablish the intellectual and moral foundations of the criminal justice system by engaging with the conceptual device of moral economy, in opposition to the idiocy of recent decades, who is willing to exercise Kantian duty and obligation: what is left of the probation system, the 21 Community Rehabilitation Companies, restorative justice, community chaplaincy and the third sector?

Probation residue

There is not much left of the probation system that began in 1907, whose rehabilitative credentials were firmly established by the 1960s (Home Office, 1962), becoming centre stage under the Criminal Justice Act 1991. After the rehabilitation revolution it continues to work with high risk offenders subjected to community orders and licence conditions. It is writing court reports to offer sentencing advice to magistrates and judges, risk assessments, allocating cases and enforcing orders and licences, undertaking parole board and public protection duties. Lying beneath revolutionary incursions is a worthy history of public service, personalist influences, a commitment to community supervision rather than punishment and custody, and human relationships as the medium of practice. In other words, there is a distinctive intellectual tradition and moral convention submerged beneath modernising accretions. Contemporary probation staff are the inheritors of a cultural tradition whose deposits can be recovered by archaeological excavation. Does the residual probation

DOI: 10.1057/9781137468468.0009

system want to safeguard its inheritance despite the unwelcome and unwarranted impositions from above? Where does it stand in relation to its past and does it want to reconstruct its ethical foundations? Or, traumatically, has it endured too much damage to recover?

Community rehabilitation companies

There are 21 community rehabilitation companies (CRC) working with thousands of low to medium risk offenders in the new dispensation: Sodexo Justice Services in partnership with NACRO (6 areas); Purple Futures (5 areas); Working Links (3 areas); The Reducing Reoffending Partnership (2 areas); MTC NOVO (2 areas); Achieving Real Change for Communities (ARCC 1 area); Geo Mercia Willowdene (1 area); and Seetec (1 area). These 21 CRCs are populated by probation staff who were transferred by April 2014. It is of interest to observe that the Sodexo website alludes to values, and that MTC Novo wants to embody the best of probation. At this inchoate stage there is no unifying statement appertaining to the intellectual and moral foundations of the CRCs to shape their work in the criminal justice system. Is this an opportunity to build such a foundation? Should they do this in consultation with the probation residue? Or are CRCs pursuing less noble priorities?

Restorative justice

Cornwell et al. (2013) advance arguments for broadening civil justice processes within the criminal justice system. Furthermore, and importantly, restorative justice is supported by the Ministry of Justice (2012d), and features as one of the aims of sentencing at s142 of the Criminal Justice Act 2003. Restorative justice requires an apology from offenders for the harms they inflict, to assume responsibility for their actions and make reparation to victims. It accepts the need for sanctions, encourages pro-social behaviour and takes a position on the implication of harms affecting victims and communities by offending. Significantly, though, it is suggested that restorative justice embodies the contours for civilising justice in a system that has become uncivilised, specifically because of state power, political interference, media influences and public responses (Blad, 2013). Restorative justice does not have hegemonic status in the

DOI: 10.1057/9781137468468.0009

criminal justice system, but it does have an ideological foothold that challenges demoralised forms of retributive and excessive punishment.

Community chaplaincy and the third sector

I conducted empirical research on community chaplaincy in Canada and England and Wales (Whitehead, 2011b). The aim was to establish an exploratory understanding of community chaplaincy in the criminal justice system of England and Wales at the end of its first decade (2001–11). Six community chaplaincy projects were visited (Leicester, Low Newton near Durham, Manchester, Leeds, Feltham and Swansea) where 22 interviews were conducted between November 2010 and April 2011. These data reveal a person-centred, theologically-informed, value-driven and voluntary-charitable organisation operating within a multi-faith ethos. It offers supportive relationships to men, women, and young people when they leave custodial institutions. Even though projects are distinguishable from other organisational domains by their faith ethos, this does not mean that all volunteers who work for community chaplaincy are people of faith or that they belong to faith communities. Community chaplaincy does not attempt to proselytise offenders. Rather, supportive relationships are offered unconditionally to people of faith and none when they leave custody. It operates with a person-in-situation mentality to counterbalance those punitive, dehumanising, and depersonalising tendencies which have colonised criminal justice. Its vision is to walk with marginalised and excluded ex-prisoners on a difficult journey because of accumulated problems compounded since unpropitious childhood experiences: family conflict, insecurity, vulnerability, impoverished education, unstable work record, substance abuse, financial problems and substandard accommodation. To people immured in adverse social circumstances community chaplaincy provides support as they return to an uncertain future in the community. Will community chaplaincy projects become assimilated into the third sector food chain of the rehabilitation revolution to ensure survival; or offer an intellectual and moral challenge?

The probation residue and 21 CRCs have an *organisational presence* in the reconfigured criminal justice system. Restorative justice, community chaplaincy and other voluntary sector organisations have an *ideological foothold*. The university sector must maintain its critical role as intellectual facilitator, through theoretical and empirical excavations, to advance

DOI: 10.1057/9781137468468.0009

thinking on foundational moral principles that transcend the ephemeral politics of contingency and disavowal. Accordingly, a Schweitzer-inspired, life-affirming philosophy, supported by Kantian moral obligation, encourages duty over utility. These are essential prerequisites to revive the moral integrity of criminal justice. The system must be sufficiently mature to accommodate sociological imagination, human understanding, feeling and moral sense as mediating filters in pursuit of criminal and social justice. The system must learn from the Hellenistic virtues of stability, balance, harmony and restraint, including the Aristotelian *mean* to steer a course between the Scylla of punitive excess and Charybdis of moral deficiency. Plato's Absolute good, his metaphysical moral foundation, is alien to our cast of mind. However, when wisdom, fortitude and temperance coalesce, there is the moral category of δικαιοσύνη (justice). Consequently, ethics, politics and justice must engage with and learn from each other. Narrowly constituted ideas of instrumental utility, fiscal calculation, punitive excess, New Public Management and blind faith in markets, have mangled the syntax of the criminal justice system and its former dialectical, if imperfect, conventions (Faulkner, 2014; Home Office, 1977). James Joyce, the radical literary artist, wanted to 'escape the nets of the market. His "usylessly" unreadable book becomes an attack on a society based on the narrow ideas of utility' (Kiberd, 2009: 20). Last, by no means least, Keynes (Skidelsky, 2003: 248) the philosopher-economist argued that what is rational is controlled by ethics and probability. In selecting a course of human action from economic theory to criminal justice, two primary decisions are required: what are the likely effects of our decisions and actions; what effects of decisions and actions make the world a better place? It is urgent and vital to advance the content of, and arguments for, moral economy to re-energise human decision making and actions throughout the criminal justice domain. Recent revolutionary events demand serious reflection, public reasoning and debate on matters fundamental and foundational to justice (Sen, 2009: 122).

These are some of the ideas from a cloud of witnesses that can be summonsed into the witness box to give evidence on morality and justice, through reconceptualising moral economy. The value of foregrounding moral economy is that it avoids reliance on the term *values*. Values have often been constructed within narrow organisational parameters and largely associated with probation (see, for example, Whitehead and Statham, 2006: 162). Moral economy, as conceptual device, is broader in scope and has richer possibilities. It is capacious enough to adopt a critical

DOI: 10.1057/9781137468468.0009

stance towards three overlapping spheres, where the first is the hegemonic *macro* neoliberal political economy. It bears repeating that political economy appertains to the state of a country, its politico-economic order, the circulation of money and goods, material objects, consumption and the circuits of investment, supply and demand, and buying and selling, in a competitive market place. Since the 1980s the resurgence of neoliberal capitalism has reconfigured the nexus of the state, finance, market and citizenship in the interests of capital accumulation and restoration of profitability *from above*. By contrast – it could not be greater – moral economy also appertains to the state of a country, but to its ethico-cultural and symbolic order, moral production and mechanisms of reproduction, and the circuits of ethico-cultural contestation. It prioritises reverence for life, living and faring well, and adopts a critical posture towards all forms of politico-economic and social organisation. Second, the primary concern of this monograph, moral economy has analytical implications at the *mezzo* organisational level and can be applied to health, education, welfare and criminal justice. Third, at the *micro* level, its human subjectivity and its complex relationship to the politico-economic system.

Moral economy, being broad in scope and application, boldly asserts that we cannot discuss ethics and justice in isolation from the politico-economic platform, its mechanisms of reproduction, and formation of human subjectivity. This does not detract from the moral obligation of *little others*, but it makes the point that this is not enough by half. Moral economy is positioned at an oblique angle to prevailing conditions and provides the intellectual resources to envision an alternative future beyond our post-political and post-ethical arrangements successfully constructed since the 1980s. The all-too-human and fundamentally necessary task is to get ourselves reorganised around a set of ethico-symbolic principles that transcend our current predicament. It is a matter of practical reason, reason exercised in its practical moral function directed towards the meaning and end of existence. A rapprochement of politics and ethics is the first vital step in creating a criminal *justice* system worthy of the name. The conceptual device of moral economy contains the intellectual resources to initiate this task.

Epilogue

Open Public Services (HM Government 2011) declared that reform in the direction of marketisation is the only way to improve public services.

DOI: 10.1057/9781137468468.0009

Political parties believe that free markets and privatisation are propitious for promoting wealth and power. Furthermore, 'open markets and free enterprise can actually promote morality' (Jones, 2015: 169). Intriguingly, this statement redefines morality by refracting it to legitimate the neoliberal order, rather than the alternative of moral economy, so we should ask what kind of morality:

▶ That allows and enables the state to manipulate the opportunity presented by the self-inflicted wound of 2007–08, the worst since the 1930s, to impose austerity on the majority and redistribute wealth and power to the elite masters of the material universe?
▶ That allows the state to bail out those who caused the crash at the expense of those who did not?
▶ That is willing to create and then live with a situation in which working people (often referred to as *ordinary* people) are forced to pick up the tab for the criminal malfeasance of the fiscal elite?
▶ That allows the state to transform public services into money-making ventures for the commercial sector, driven by crude ideology, not evidence, that private is better than public?

Specifically, what kind of morality:

▶ Allows and enables the state to turn its repressive criminal justice apparatus against the poorest sections of society (Prison Reform Trust, 2014) rather than serious harms caused by the powerful (targeting benefit fraud by the demonised other rather than tax evasion of the Establishment's protected species)?
▶ Allows the state to live with the preventable pathologies attendant on the neoliberal order, perpetuating policies that exacerbate not ameliorate those human problems elucidated by Wilkinson and Pickett (2009), from physical and mental ill-health to crime and punishment?
▶ Aggressively pursues organisational modernisation through revolutionary activity that banishes intellectual and moral resources in a tactical display of will to power?

This 'morality' is epiphenomenon to the capitalist platform, not intrinsic to moral economy. The state's morality, the morality of choice, of open markets and free enterprise as the outriders of neoliberal capitalism, is a pseudo-morality, a false god, a gross distortion. This is not the morality of moral economy that begins with Schweitzer's reverence for life and ends

DOI: 10.1057/9781137468468.0009

with the reunification of politics and ethics to support a new universal world order that reorders the macro, mezzo and micro dimensions of existence. Moral economy advances a systematically new anthropological starting point of mutual coexistence in the polis. Moral economy is μετανοια – a radical change of heart and mind.

Note

1 By applying the terminology of Lacan and Žižek we are invited to reflect on the concept of *little others* to compensate for the sense of loss after 2010–15 (Žižek, 1992; 2006). Evidentially the old meanings, structures and conventions that comprised the system have been eroded. Governmental attachment to, and support for, probation has withered, witnessed by imposed privatisation. The former things have passed away, but little others offer some hope, no matter how tenuous.

DOI: 10.1057/9781137468468.0009

References

Allen, F.A. (1981) *The Decline of the Rehabilitative Ideal: Penal Policy and Social Purpose* (New Haven and London: Yale University Press).

Allen, K. (2004) *Max Weber: A Critical Introduction* (London: Pluto).

American Friends Service Committee (1971) *Struggle for Justice: A Report on Crime and Punishment in America* (New York: Farrar Straus and Giroux).

Aristotle (2000) *Nicomachean Ethics*, Translated and Edited by R. Crisp (Cambridge: Cambridge University Press).

Armstrong, K. (2006) *A Short History of Myth* (Edinburgh: Canongate).

Arrighi, G. (2010) *The Long Twentieth Century: Money, Power, and the Origin of Our Times* (London and New York: Verso).

Audit Commission (1989) *Promoting Value for Money in the Probation Service* (London: HMSO).

Badiou, A. (2003) *Saint Paul: The Foundations of Universalism* (Stanford: Stanford University Press).

Bauman, Z. (2001) *The Individualised Society* (Cambridge: Polity).

Bell, E. (2011) *Criminal Justice and Neoliberalism* (Houndmills, UK: Palgrave Macmillan).

Berdyaev, N. (1935) *The Fate of Man in the Modern World* (London: SCM).

Berman, G. and Dar, A. (2013) *Prison Population Statistics* (London: House of Commons Library).

DOI: 10.1057/9781137468468.0010

Bethge, E. (1970) *Dietrich Bonhoeffer: A Biography* (London: Collins).

Blad, J. (2013) 'Civilisation of Criminal Justice: Restorative Justice amongst other Strategies' in: D.J. Cornwell, J. Blad and M. Wright (eds) *Civilising Justice: An International Restorative Agenda for Penal Reform* (Sherfield-on-Loddon: Waterside Press).

Block, F. (2006) 'A moral economy', *The Nation*, 20 (March), 16–19.

Blumenfeld, B. (2001) *The Political Paul: Justice, Democracy and Kingship in a Hellenistic Framework* (London and New York: Sheffield Academic Press).

Bobbitt, P. (2002) *The Shield of Achilles: War, Peace and the Course of History* (London and New York: Penguin).

Bonhoeffer, D. (1955) *Ethics*, E. Bethge (ed.) (London and New York: Macmillan).

Bonhoeffer, D. (1963) *The Communion of Saints* (London: Harper Row).

Bonhoeffer, D. (1966) *Christology* (London: Harper Row).

Bonhoeffer, D. (1971) *Letters and Papers from Prison*, E. Bethge (ed.) (London: SCM).

Booth, W.J. (1994) 'On the idea of the moral economy', *The American Political Science Review*, 88 (3), 653–67.

Bottoms, A.E. and Preston, R.H. (1980) (eds) *The Coming Penal Crisis: A Criminological and Theological Exploration* (Edinburgh: Scottish Academic Press).

Box, S. (1987) *Recession, Crime and Punishment* (Houndmills UK: Macmillan).

Brody, S. (1976) *The Effectiveness of Sentencing* (London: HMSO).

Buber, M. (1970) *I and Thou* (Edinburgh: T. and T. Clark).

Burke, L. and Collett, (2014) *Delivering Rehabilitation: The Politics, Governance and Control of Probation* (Abingdon: Routledge).

Burnett, R., Baker, K. and Roberts, C. (2007) 'Assessment, Supervision and Intervention: Fundamental Practice in Probation', in: L. Gelsthorpe and R. Morgan (eds) *Handbook of Probation* (Cullompton: Willan).

Burrow, J. (2009) *A History of Histories: Epics, Chronicles, Romances and Inquiries from Herodotus and Thucydides to the Twentieth Century* (London and New York: Penguin).

Cabinet Office (2010) *Modernising Commissioning: Increasing the Role of Charities, Social Enterprises, Mutuals and Cooperatives in Public Service Delivery* (London: Cabinet Office).

Canton, R. (2007) 'Probation and the tragedy of punishment', *Howard Journal*, 46 (3), 236–54.

DOI: 10.1057/9781137468468.0010

Canton, R. (2011) *Probation: Working with Offenders* (Abingdon: Routledge).

Carter, P. (2003) *Managing Offenders, Reducing Crime: A New Approach* (London: Home Office).

Carter, P. (2007) *Securing the Future: Proposals for the Efficient and Sustainable Use of Custody in England and Wales* (London: Ministry of Justice).

Cavadino, M. and Dignan, J. (2006) *Penal Systems: A Comparative Approach* (London: Sage).

Chambers, M. (2013) *Expanding Payment by Results: Strategic Choices and Recommendations* (London: Policy Exchange).

Chernomas, R. and Hudson, I. (2007) *Social Murder and Other Shortcomings of Conservative Economics* (Winnipeg: Arbeiter Ring Publishing).

Chomsky, N. (1999) *Profit over People: Neoliberalism and Global Order* (New York: Seven Stories Press).

Chui, W.H. and Nellis, M. (2003) (eds) *Moving Probation Forward: Evidence, Arguments and Practice* (Harlow: Pearson Longman).

Clarke, P. (2004) *Hope and Glory: Britain 1900–2000* 2nd edition (London and New York: Penguin).

Conservative Party (2008) *Prisons with a Purpose: Our Sentencing and Rehabilitation Revolution to Break the Cycle of Crime, Security Agenda Policy Green Paper Number 4* (London: Conservative Party).

Copleston, F. ([1946] 2003) *Greece and Rome, A History of Philosophy Volume 1* (London: Continuum).

Copleston, F. ([1975] 2003) *French Philosophy, A History of Philosophy Volume 9* (London: Continuum).

Cornwell, D.J., Blad, J. and Wright, M. (2013) (eds) *Civilising Justice: An International Restorative Agenda for Penal Reform* (Sherfield-on-Loddon: Waterside Press).

Crouch, C. (2011) *The Strange Non-death of Neoliberalism* (Cambridge: Polity).

Cullen, B. (1979) *Hegel's Social and Political Thought* (London and New York: Gill and Macmillan).

Cullen, M.J. (1975) *The Statistical Movement in Early Victorian Britain: The Foundations of Empirical Social Research* (Hassocks Sussex: The Harvester Press).

Cullen, F.T. and Gilbert, K.E. (1982) *Reaffirming Rehabilitation* (Cincinnati: Anderson Publishing).

DOI: 10.1057/9781137468468.0010

Davies, M., Croall, H. and Tyrer, J. (2010) *Criminal Justice* 4th edition (Harlow: Pearson).

De Angelis, M. (2007) *The Beginning of History: Value Struggles and Global Capitalism* (London: Pluto).

Dillistone, F.W. (1982) *The Christian Understanding of Atonement* (London: SCM).

Douzinas, C. (2013) *Philosophy and Resistance in the Crisis: Greece and the Future of Europe* (Cambridge: Polity).

Drew, P. (1992) 'The probation service: a few valedictory comments', *Probation Journal*, 39 (2), 92–94.

Dumas, A. (1971) *Dietrich Bonhoeffer: Theologian of Reality* (London: SCM).

Duménil, G. and Lévy, D. (2004) *Capital Resurgent: Roots of the Neoliberal Revolution* (Cambridge and London: Harvard University Press).

Durkheim, E. (1984) *The Division of Labour in Society*, Introduction by L. Coser, Translated by W.D. Halls (Basingstoke: Macmillan).

Dyer, C. (2000) *Everyday Life in Medieval England* (London: Hambledon and London).

Eagleton, T. (2009) *Trouble with Strangers: A Study of Ethics* (Chichester: Wiley-Blackwell).

Eagleton, T. (2014) *Culture and the Death of God* (New Haven and London: Yale University Press).

Elliott, A. (2005) 'Psychoanalytic Social Theory' in: A. Harrington (2005) (ed.) *Modern Social Theory: An Introduction* (Oxford and New York: Oxford University Press).

Farrall, S. and Jennings, W. (2014) 'Thatcherism and Crime: The Beast that Never Roared? in: S. Farrall and C. Hay (eds) *The Legacy of Thatcherism: Assessing and Exploring Thatcherite Social and Economic Policies* (Oxford: Published for the British Academy by Oxford University Press).

Faulkner, D. (1993) Government emphasis on criminalisation and punishment has destroyed old rules and values and created a void in the justice system: The result is anger and rising crime (*Guardian Newspaper*, 12 November).

Faulkner, D. (2014) *Servant of the Crown: A Civil Servant's Story of Criminal Justice and Public Service Reform* (Sherfield-on-Loddon: Waterside Press).

Faulkner, D. and Burnett, R. (2012) *Where Next for Criminal Justice?* (Bristol: The Policy Press).

DOI: 10.1057/9781137468468.0010

Fenton, S. (1984) *Durkheim and Modern Sociology* (Cambridge and New York: Cambridge University Press).

Folkard, S., Fowles, A.J., McWilliams, B.C., Smith, D.D., Smith, D.E. and Walmsley, G.R. (1974) *IMPACT Volume 1, The Design of the Probation Experiment and the Interim Evaluation* (London: HMSO).

Folkard, S., Smith, D.E. and Smith, D.D (1976) *IMPACT Volume 2, The Results of the Experiment* (London: HMSO).

Fullwood, C. (1994) 'Policy and Management Implications' in: J. Stewart, D. Smith and G. Stewart with C. Fullwood (eds), *Understanding Offending Behaviour* (Harlow: Longman).

Galbraith, J.K. (2008) *The Predator State: How Conservatives Abandoned the Free Market and Why Liberals Should Too* (New York and London: Free Press).

Garland, D. (1985) *Punishment and Welfare: A History of Penal Strategies* (Aldershot: Gower).

Garland, D. (2001) *The Culture of Control: Crime and Social Disorder in Contemporary Society* (Oxford and New York: Oxford University Press).

Hall, S. (2012) *Theorizing Crime and Deviance: A New Perspective* (London: Sage).

Hall, S., Critcher, C., Jefferson, T. and Clarke, J. (1978) *Policing the Crisis: Mugging, the State and Law and Order* (Houndmills UK: Macmillan).

Hall, S. and Jacques, M. (1983) (eds) *The Politics of Thatcherism* (London: Lawrence and Wishart).

Hand, S. (1989) (ed.) *The Levinas Reader* (Oxford: Blackwell).

Harari, Y.N. (2014) *Sapiens: A Brief History of Humankind* (London: Harvill Secker).

Harrington, A. (2005) (ed.) *Modern Social Theory: An Introduction* (Oxford and New York: Oxford University Press).

Harvey, D. (2010) *The Enigma of Capital and the Crises of Capitalism* (London: Profile Books).

Hastings, M. (2013) *Catastrophe: Europe Goes to War 1914* (London: William Collins).

Haxby, D. (1978) *Probation: A Changing Service* (London: Constable).

Hedges, C. (2010) *Death of the Liberal Class* (New York: Nation Books).

H.M. Government (2010a) *Building a Stronger Society: A Strategy for Voluntary and Community Groups, Charities and Social Enterprises* (London: Cabinet Office).

H.M. Government (2010b) *The Coalition: Our Programme for Government* (London: H.M. Government).

DOI: 10.1057/9781137468468.0010

H.M. Government (2011) *Open Public Services*, CM 8145 (London: The Stationery Office).

Hobsbawm, E. (1977) *The Age of Revolution: Europe 1989–1848* (London: Abacus).

Hobsbawm, E. (1994) *Age of Extremes: The Short Twentieth Century 1914–1991* (London: Michael Joseph).

Home Office (1962) *Report of the Departmental Committee on the Probation Service* (Morison Committee), Cmnd 1650 (London: HMSO).

Home Office (1977) *A Review of Criminal Justice Policy 1976* (London: HMSO).

Home Office (1995) *Strengthening Punishment in the Community: A Consultation Document*, Cmnd 2780 (London: HMSO).

Home Office (1999) *Increasing Confidence in Community Sentences: The Results of Two Demonstration Projects*, Research Study 194 (London: Home Office).

Home Office (2007) *Re-offending by Adults: Results from the 2004 Cohort* (London: Home Office).

Homer, S. (2005) *Jacques Lacan* (London and New York: Routledge).

Hood, C. (1991) 'A public management for all seasons', *Public Administration*, 69 (Spring), 3–19.

House of Commons Justice Committee (14.1.2014) *Crime Reduction Policies: A Coordinated Approach? Interim Report on the Government's Transforming Rehabilitation Programme*, Twelfth Report of Session 2013-13 (London: House of Commons).

Hume, D. ([1777] 1983) *An Enquiry Concerning the Principles of Morals*, Edited by J.B. Schneewind (Indianapolis and Cambridge: Hackett Publishing Company).

Humphrey, (1987) *The Implications of the FMI for the Probation Service* (Department of Accounting and Finance: University of Manchester).

Jameson, F. (1991) *Postmodernism, or, the Cultural Logic of Late Capitalism* (London: Verso).

Jenkins, D. (2002) *The Calling of a Cuckoo: Not Quite an Autobiography* (London and New York: Continuum).

Jenkins, D. (2004) *Market Whys and Human Wherefores: Thinking Again about Markets, Politics and People* (London and New York: Continuum).

Jones, E. (1968) *Profiles of the Prophets* (Oxford: The Religious Education Press).

DOI: 10.1057/9781137468468.0010

Jones, O. (2015) *The Establishment: And How They Get Away With It* (Harmondsworth: Penguin).

Jones, T. and Newburn, T. (2007) *Policy Transfer and Criminal Justice: Exploring US Influence over British Crime Control Policy* (Maidenhead: Open University Press).

Kant, I. ([1785] 2005) *The Moral Law: Groundwork of the Metaphysics of Morals* (Abingdon: Routledge).

Kelly, J.N.D. (1968) *Early Christian Doctrines* 4th edition (London: Adam and Charles Black).

Kelly, G.B. and Nelson, F.B. (2003) *The Cost of Moral Leadership: The Spirituality of Dietrich Bonhoeffer* (Grand Rapids and Cambridge: Eerdmans).

Kennedy, H. (2005) *Just Law: The Changing Face of Justice – And Why It Matters to Us All* (London: Vintage).

Kenny, A. (2010) *A New History of Western Philosophy: In Four Parts* (Oxford and New York: Clarendon).

Kiberd, D. (2009) *Ulysses and Us: The Art of Everyday Living* (London: Faber and Faber).

Klein, G. (2014) *Seeing What Other's Don't: The Remarkable Ways We Gain Insights* (New York: Public Affairs).

Knight-Markiegi, A. and Quinn, A. (2013) *Comparing Payment by Results Across Public Services and in Housing Related Support* (London: Sitra).

Küng, H. (1977) *On Being A Christian* (London: Collins).

Küng, H. (1998) *A Global Ethic for Global Politics and Economics* (Oxford and New York: Oxford University Press).

Lacan, J. (2001) *Écrits* (Abingdon: Routledge).

Lanchester, J. (2010) *Whoops: Why Everyone Owes Everyone and No One Can Pay* (London: Penguin).

Lawson, N. (2013) 'Against all the odds: the economic legacy of Thatcherism', *The Sunday Times Commemorative Edition* (14 April) 12–14.

Lipton, D., Martinson, R. and Wilks, J. (1975) *Effectiveness of Correctional Treatment* (Springfield Massachusetts: Praeger).

Lloyd, C. (1986) *Responses to SNOP* (Institute of Criminology: University of Cambridge).

MacIntyre, A. (1967) *A Short History of Ethics* (London: Routledge and Kegan Paul).

McMurtry, J. (2002) *Value Wars: The Global Market versus the Life Economy* (London: Pluto).

DOI: 10.1057/9781137468468.0010

McNeil, F. and Weaver, B. (2010) *Changing Lives? Desistance Research and Offender Management*, The Scottish Centre for Crime and Justice Research, Report Number 03/2010 (University of Glasgow and Strathclyde).

Mair, G. and Burke, L. (2012) *Redemption, Rehabilitation and Risk Management: A History of Probation* (Abingdon: Routledge).

Marquand, D. (2014) *Mammon's Kingdom: An Essay on Britain, Now* (London and New York: Allen Lane).

Martinson, R. (1974) 'What Works? Questions about prison reform', *The Public Interest*, 35, 22–54.

Maruna, S. (2001) *Making Good: How Ex-Convicts Reform and Rebuild their Lives* (Washington, D.C: American Psychological Association).

Mawby, R. and Worrall, A. (2013) *Doing Probation Work: Identity in a Criminal Justice Occupation* (Abingdon: Routledge).

Mead, R. (2014) *The Road to Middlemarch: My Life with George Eliot* (London: Granta).

Meštrović, S.G. (1997) *Postemotional Society* (London: Sage).

Metaxas, E. (2010) *Bonhoeffer Pastor, Martyr, Prophet, Spy: A Righteous Gentile vs. the Third Reich* (Nashville: Thomas Nelson).

Metzger, B.M. and Coogan, M.D. (1993) *The Oxford Companion to the Bible* (Oxford and New York: Oxford University Press).

Milbank, J. (2010) 'Paul against Biopolitics' in: J. Milbank, S. Žižek and C. Davis (eds), *Paul's New Moment: Continental Philosophy and the Future of Christian Theology* (Michigan: Brazos Press).

Milbank, J., Žižek, S. and Davis, C (2010) *Paul's New Moment: Continental Philosophy and the Future of Christian Theology* (Michigan: Brazos Press).

Ministry of Justice (2010) *Breaking the Cycle: Effective Punishment, Rehabilitation and Sentencing of Offenders* (London: Ministry of Justice).

Ministry of Justice (2011) *Competition Strategy for Offender Services* (London: Ministry of Justice).

Ministry of Justice (2012a) *Punishment and Reform: Effective Community Sentences*, Consultation Paper CP8/2012 (London: Ministry of Justice).

Ministry of Justice (2012b) *Punishment and Reform: Effective Probation Services*, Consultation Paper CP7/2012 (London: Ministry of Justice).

Ministry of Justice (2012c) *Swift and Sure Justice: The Government's Plans for Reform of the Criminal Justice System*, CM 8388 (London: Ministry of Justice).

DOI: 10.1057/9781137468468.0010

Ministry of Justice (2012d) *Restorative Justice Action Plan for the Criminal Justice System* (London: Ministry of Justice).

Ministry of Justice Analytical Series (2013a) *Transforming Rehabilitation: A Summary of Evidence on Reducing Reoffending* (London: Ministry of Justice).

Ministry of Justice (2013b) *Transforming Rehabilitation: A Revolution in the Way We Manage Offenders*, Consultation Paper CP1/2013 (London: Ministry of Justice).

Ministry of Justice (2013c) *Transforming Rehabilitation: A Strategy for Reform*, CM 8619, Response to Consultation CP (R) 16/2013 (London: Ministry of Justice).

Ministry of Justice (2013d) *Target Operating Manual: Rehabilitation Programme* (London: Ministry of Justice).

Ministry of Justice (2013e) *Best in the Business Bidding to Rehabilitate Offenders* (London: Ministry of Justice).

Ministry of Justice (2013f) *Statistical Notice: Interim Re-conviction Figures for the Peterborough and Doncaster Payment by Results Pilots* (London: Ministry of Justice).

Ministry of Justice (2013g) *Story of the Prison Population 1993–2012 England and Wales* (London: Ministry of Justice).

Mounier, E. (1952) *Personalism* (Notre Dame: University of Notre Dame Press).

Mozley, E.N. (1950) *The Theology of Albert Schweitzer for Christian Enquirers* (London: Adam and Charles Black).

Mumford, L. (1940) 'The corruption of liberalism', *The New Republic*, 29 April, 568–72.

Myers, T. (2003) *Slavoj Žižek* (Abingdon: Routledge).

National Audit Office (1989) *Home Office: Control and Management of Probation Services in England and Wales*, HC 377, 1988/89 Session (London: HMSO).

Outram, D. (2013) *The Enlightenment* 3rd edition (Cambridge: Cambridge University Press).

Pagden, A. (2013) *The Enlightenment: And Why It Still Matters* (Oxford: Oxford University Press).

Piketty, T. (2014) *Capital in the Twenty-First Century* (Cambridge Massachusetts and London: The Belknap Press of Harvard University).

Pinkard, T. (2000) *Hegel: A Biography* (Cambridge: Cambridge University Press).

DOI: 10.1057/9781137468468.0010

Pinker, S. (2015) *The Village Effect: Why Face-To-Face Contact Matters* (London: Atlantic).

Plant, R. (1973) *Hegel* (London: George Allen and Unwin).

Plato (1974) *Republic* (Harmondsworth: Penguin).

Polanyi, K. (2001) *The Great Transformation: The Political and Economic Origins of Our Time* (Boston: Beacon Press).

Prison Reform Trust (2014) *Bromley Briefings Prison Factfile* (London: PRT).

Raines, J. (2002) (ed.) *Marx on Religion* (Philadelphia: Temple University Press).

Reiner, R. (2007) *Law and Order: An Honest Citizen's Guide to Crime and Control* (Cambridge: Polity).

Robinson, J.A.T. (1973) *The Human Face of God* (London: SCM).

Roudinesco, E. (2014) *Lacan: In Spite of Everything* (London and New York: Verso).

Russell, L.M. (1941) *The Path to Reconstruction: A Brief Introduction to Albert Schweitzer's Philosophy of Civilization* (London: Adam and Charles Black).

Sandel, M. (2009) *Justice: What's the Right Thing to Do?* (London and New York: Penguin).

Sandel, M. (2012) *What Money Can't Buy: The Moral Limits of Markets* (London and New York: Allen Lane).

Sayer, A. (2000) 'Moral economy and political economy', *Studies in Political Economy*, 61 (Spring Issue), 79–104, Lancaster University.

Schneewind, J.B. (2003) (ed.) *Moral Philosophy from Montaigne to Kant* (Cambridge: Cambridge University Press).

Schweitzer, A. (1929) *Civilisation and Ethics: The Philosophy of Civilisation, Part 2* 2nd edition (London: A. and C. Black).

Schweitzer, A. (1955) *On the Edge of the Primeval Forest* (London: A. and C. Black).

Schweitzer, A. (1961) *The Decay and Restoration of Civilisation: The Philosophy of Civilisation, Part 1* (London: Unwin).

Schweitzer, A. (1962) *My Childhood and Youth* (London: Unwin).

Scott, J.C. (1976) *The Moral Economy of the Peasant: Rebellion and Subsistence in South East Asia* (USA: Yale University Press).

Seaver, G. (1947) *Albert Schweitzer: The Man and His Mind* (London: A. and C. Black).

Sen, A. (2009) *The Idea of Justice* (London and New York: Allen Lane).

DOI: 10.1057/9781137468468.0010

Shaw, R. and Haines, K. (1989) *The Criminal Justice System: A Central Role for the Probation Service*, Institute of Criminology: University of Cambridge.

Sinnerbrink, R.S. (2008) 'The Hegelian "Night of the World": Žižek on subjectivity, negativity, and universality', *International Journal of Žižek Studies*, 2 (2), 1–21.

Skidelsky, R. (2003) *John Maynard Keynes 1883–1946: Economist, Philosopher, Statesman* (London and New York: Penguin).

Smith, A. ([1759] 2009) *The Theory of Moral Sentiments*, Introduction by A. Sen (London and New York: Penguin).

Smith, A. (1776) An Inquiry Into the Nature and Causes of the Wealth of Nations.

Solomon, E., Eades, C., Garside, R. and Rutherford, M. (2007) *Ten Years of Criminal Justice under Labour: An Independent Audit* (London: Centre for Crime and Justice Studies, King's College, London).

Squires, P. and Lee, J. (2013) (eds) *Criminalisation and Advanced Marginality: Critically Exploring the Work of Loic Wacquant* (Bristol: Policy Press).

Standing, G. (2011) *The Precariat: The New Dangerous Class* (London: Bloomsbury).

Statham, R. (2014) (ed.) *The Golden Age of Probation: Market v Mission* (Sherfield-on-Loddon, Waterside Press).

Stewart, G. (2013) *Bang! A History of Britain in the 1980s* (London: Atlantic Books).

Stone, L. (1987) *The Past and the Present Revisited* (Abingdon: Routledge).

Taylor, C. (2007) *A Secular Age* (Cambridge Massachusetts and London: The Belknap Press of Harvard University).

Thatcher, M. (1995) *The Path to Power* (London: Harper Collins).

Thomas, K. (2009) *The Ends of Life: Roads to Fulfilment in Early Modern England* (Oxford: Oxford University Press).

Thompson, E.P. (1971) 'The moral economy of the English crowd in the eighteenth century', *Past and Present*, 50, 76–136.

Tönnies, F. (2002) *Community and Society: Gemeinschaft and Gesellschaft* (Mineola, New York: Dover Publications).

Tonry, M. (2004) *Punishment and Politics: Evidence and Emulation in the Making of English Crime Control Policy* (Cullompton: Willan).

Valier, C. (2002) *Theories of Crime and Punishment* (Harlow: Longman).

Varoufakis, Y. (2013) *The Global Minotaur: America, Europe and the Future of the Global Economy* (London and New York: Zed Books).

DOI: 10.1057/9781137468468.0010

Wacquant, L. (2009) *Punishing the Poor: The Neoliberal Government of Social Insecurity* (Durham and London: Duke University Press).

Weber, M. (1968) *Economy and Society: An Outline of Interpretive Sociology*, 3 volumes, Edited by Guenther Roth and Claus Wittich (New York: Bedminster Press).

Whitehead, P. (2010) *Exploring Modern Probation: Social Theory and Organisational Complexity* (Bristol: Policy Press).

Whitehead, P. (2011a) 'Breaking the cycle or recycling errors: critical comment on proposals for criminal justice reform', *Critical Social Policy*, 31 (4), 628–39.

Whitehead, P. (2011b) *Evaluation Report of Research at Six Community Chaplaincy Projects in England and Wales* (Community Chaplaincy Association and Teesside University).

Whitehead, P. (2015) 'Payment by results: the materialist reconstruction of criminal justice', *International Journal of Sociology and Social Policy*, 35 (5/6), 290–305.

Whitehead, P. and Crawshaw, P. (2012) 'Introduction: A Preliminary Mapping of the Terrain' in: P. Whitehead and P. Crawshaw (eds) *Organising Neoliberalism: Markets, Privatisation and Justice* (London and New York: Anthem Press).

Whitehead, P. and Statham, R. (2006) *The History of Probation: Politics, Power and Cultural Change 1876–2005* (Crayford: Shaw and Sons).

Whitehead, P. and Thompson, J. (2004) *Knowledge and the Probation Service: Raising Standards for Trainees, Assessors and Practitioners* (Chichester: Wiley).

Whitfield, D. (2006) *New Labour's Attack on Public Services: Modernisation by Marketisation* (Nottingham: Spokesman Books).

Whitfield, D. (2012) *In Place of Austerity: Reconstructing the Economy, State and Public Services* (Nottingham: Spokesman Books).

Whittingdon, C. (1988) 'Literature review: the efficacy and performance assessment debate', *British Journal of Social Work*, 18 (2).

Wiegratz, J. (2010) 'Fake capitalism? The dynamics of neoliberal moral restructuring and pseudo-development: the case of Uganda', *Review of African Political Economy*, 37 (124), 123–37.

Wiegratz, J. (2011) 'The morality of economic malpractice and crime in neoliberal capitalism', *BISA Annual Conference*, Manchester, 27–29 April.

Wilkinson, R. and Pickett, K. (2009) *The Spirit Level: Why More Equal Societies Almost Always Do Better* (London and New York: Allen Lane).

DOI: 10.1057/9781137468468.0010

Windlesham (1993) *Responses to Crime, Volume 2: Penal Policy in the Making* (Oxford and New York: Clarendon).

Windlesham (2001) *Responses to Crime, Volume 4: Dispensing Justice* (Oxford and New York: Clarendon).

Winlow, S. and Hall, S. (2013) *Rethinking Social Exclusion: The End of the Social?* (London: Sage).

Wood, C. (1991) *The End of Punishment: Christian Perspectives on the Crisis in Criminal Justice* (Edinburgh Centre for Theology and Public Issues: St. Andrews Press).

Wright, N.T. (2009) *Justification: God's Plan and Paul's Vision* (London: SPCK).

Žižek, S. (1992) *Looking Awry: An Introduction to Jacques Lacan through Popular Culture* (Cambridge Massachusetts and London: The MIT Press).

Žižek, S. (2006) *How To Read Lacan* (London: Granta Books).

Žižek, S. (2008) *The Fragile Absolute, or, Why Is the Christian Legacy Worth Fighting for?* (London and New York: Verso).

Žižek, S. (2010) 'A Meditation on Michelangelo's *Christ on the Cross*' in: J. Milbank., S. Žižek and C. Davis (eds), *Paul's New Moment: Continental Philosophy and the Future of Christian Theology* (Michigan: Brazos Press).

Žižek, S. (2014) *Trouble in Paradise: Communism after the End of History* (London: Allen Lane).

DOI: 10.1057/9781137468468.0010

Index

DOI: 10.1057/9781137468468.0011

DOI: 10.1057/9781137468468.0011

Printed by Printforce, the Netherlands